TALL ENOUGH
TO COACH

TALL ENOUGH TO COACH

Elements of Leadership for Coaching and Life

by Marsha Sharp

WITH EMILY F. SHARP

BRIGHT SKY PRESS

Box 416, Albany, Texas 76430

Text copyright © 2004 by Marsha Sharp and Emily F. Sharp

10 9 8 7 6 5 4 3 2 1

Library of Congress Cataloging-in-Publication Data

Sharp, Marsha.
Tall enough to coach / by Marsha Sharp and Emily F. Sharp.
p. cm.
Includes bibliographical references.
ISBN 1-931721-46-7 (alk. paper)
1. Basketball-Coaching. 2. Sharp, Marsha. 3. Texas Tech University-
Basketball. I.
Sharp, Emily F. (Emily Foreman), 1961- II. Title.

GV885.3.S53 2004
796.323'07'7-dc22

2004058522

Jacket and book design by DJ Stout
and Julie Savasky, Pentagram, Austin.

TABLE OF CONTENTS

PREFACE

WEST TEXAS IS IN MY BLOOD. EVEN THOUGH I WAS BORN IN WASHINGTON AND lived in New Mexico as a child, West Texas is home to me. It is a place which possesses a unique, two-hearted beauty. From its breathtaking sunsets, to its brilliant starry nights, to its serpentine fields of snow-white cotton, a person cannot help but feel the opportunity here. These surroundings repeat themselves in the personalities of true West Texans—there is a vastness about them in terms of their can-do spirit, their genuine friendship, their untiring work ethic, and their close-knit relationships. Under girding all of these traits is an intense faith which guides most major decisions. Perhaps that confidence in God stems from centuries of farmers' prayers each planting season; it takes faith to plant a seed and nurture it through all kinds of weather. As a child, I spent many hours on this land—either chopping cotton, caring for cattle, or harvesting our family's vegetable garden. We even raised pigs! On many mornings, my entire family would go to the farm, load pigs into a trailer and head to Plainview, so the pigs could be made into Jimmy Dean sausage. Then, we would go home and get ready for school. Later, when I would play "This Little Piggy Went to Market" with my baby nephews' toes, I would remember those early morning trips to the pig farm. Making a life from the land was a full time job indeed, but I came to appreciate the strong family ties it strengthened with every passing season.

West Texas people, against a West Texas background, make for a beautiful thing. That the landscape is level all around makes no one really that much taller or better than the other; you are who you are. But, if you live in West Texas, you'd better deal honestly, because folks can see you coming for miles. It is a land of possibility and infinite skies; consequently, it's a terrific place to have big dreams.

Many of these dreams are played out along Interstate 27, which runs north and south through this land. During the fall on Friday nights, the sky is aglow with the lights of small town football stadiums sporadically placed along the road. A love of athletic competition is legendary here, not only on the football fields, but also in the hundreds of basketball gyms which become places of community for all kinds of folks. As you drive along the highway, it is not uncommon to be greeted by billboards proclaiming the town's champions of years current and past—a testament to a single event that put a small town "on the map," if only for a season. Tulia, Plainview, Hale Center, Abernathy, Lockney, Slaton, and all the towns in between share a

bees take trophy

Wayland's Queen Bees captured the Phillips Invitational trophy Saturday night, dumping host Phillips 66-63 in the title game. Tina Slinker scored 15 points while Breena Caldwell came in second with 14. Marie Korcurek had 10 and Lynn Davis added nine.

On Friday the Bees crushed John F. Kennedy's J.V. 92-36 as Leann Waddell scored 20 points. In the first game, which was on Thursday, the Bees defeated Wichita State, 80-36. Waddell and Korcurek both had twelve points.

queen bees
WBC's Queen Bees had much to be thankful for over the Thanksgiving holidays. They took a top ranking in the Phillips Invitational tournament and brough

The Wayland Baptist College Queen Bees under the leadership of Coach Sharp (left).

passion for sports, especially for basketball. I am a product of this passion and have spent my life pursuing its elusive dreams.

Some of the most significant events in my life have occurred in West Texas, especially within a seventy-five mile radius of Lubbock. My journey into the world of sports began north of Lubbock at Tulia Jr. High School, where I began playing basketball in 1964. My love of the game continued into high school, where I was on the Tulia Hornette basketball team. Women's basketball was a six-man game then, and I played both forward and guard which allowed me to play on both ends of the court and be part of all of the action. I was fortunate and proud to be named to the All-District basketball team my senior year.

After graduating high school in 1970, I decided to attend Wayland Baptist College in Plainview, a community just twenty-five miles south of Tulia. Plainview was not only home of Jimmy Dean, but also home of the storied Wayland Flying Queens basketball team. I wasn't sure what I was going to do with my life, but I thought it had something to do with basketball. I became Queens' manager while completing my undergraduate degree in physical education and English. I was a sophomore at Wayland when I discovered a sobering truth. Flying Queen Head Coach, Harley Redin, looked me in the eye one day and said, "I know how much you want to play collegiate basketball, but you're just too short and too slow." I didn't hear much beyond that. I wasn't tall enough to be a Queen! I truly loved the game and wanted to play so badly. I was devastated. I even discussed my future with Dr. Roy McClung, the president of Wayland, to see if he could change Coach Redin's mind. Not so. Thankfully, however, Coach Redin didn't give up on me entirely. He told me that while I wasn't good enough to play, I might have what it took to be a coach. He asked me if I would coach the Queen Bees, the Flying Queens junior varsity team. I gulped and said yes. That was the beginning of my coaching career.

I was privileged to coach an outstanding group of talented, fun-loving women who had much patience with me as a rookie. I learned the value of creating team chemistry through that experience as many of the players have remained close friends through the years. Because we played some of our games through the holiday season, it was not uncommon for the Queen Bees to fill my parents' home in Tulia for Thanksgiving or Spring Break, visits which forged the threads of relationships that extended to the basketball court. In 1973, the Queen Bees ended the season with 25 wins and 8 losses. I began to see coaching as both a challenging and rewarding profession—and it didn't matter how tall or how fast I happened to be!

The next year, the Flying Queens came under the leadership of Coach Dean Weese who would become one of women's basketball's greatest champions. Because I felt a calling to pursue a coaching career, I asked him if I could manage the Flying Queens and be in the shadow of his expertise. He agreed and that began a relationship that continues to this day. Little did I know that, years later, I would depend on him not only as my mentor, but also as the older brother of Linden Weese, my faithful assistant coach for the Lady Raiders for more than two decades.

The Wayland Flying Queen experience afforded many opportunities to see women's basketball at its best. In 1974, Janice Beach, Carolyn Bush, Pearl Worrell and Brenda Moeller were all members of that National Amateur Athletic Union Tournament title team, in addition to being named All-Americans. I remember that the *Wayland College Trail Blazer*, the school's newspaper, had this to say about the victory: "At last, the meaning of 'Queen' was revealed—capable of facing battle with her head held high regardless of the final outcome because she would give her all—for herself, for her teammates, and her fans." I have thought of those lofty ideas many times throughout my career and am grateful for the chance to have been a small part of the Flying Queens' history.

Following my graduation from Wayland in 1974, I decided to stay on one more season with the Queen Bees while pursuing a master's degree in education at West Texas State University. We had a 19–2 record that year and were runner-up in the state collegiate tournament. I applied for and received

Coach Sharp with her mentor, Jeannine McHaney.

an offer for the head basketball coaching position at Lockney, Texas, a town just east of Plainview. It is interesting to note that nine other female Wayland graduates were coaching in the surrounding West Texas towns. The Wayland Flying Queens influence cannot be underestimated when studying women's basketball history. It is truly an amazing phenomenon not only for our sport, but also for the initial rise of women's leadership through-out the country.

I can honestly say that my experience at Lockney High School was a significant turning point in my career. The people there were wonderful and took a twenty-two year old novice into their community and made me feel like I had been there forever. I had terrific kids who wanted more than anything to be successful and to please their coaches and teachers. While they learned the game, I learned to coach and how to compete against other West Texas powerhouses like the Abernathy Antelopes and the Tulia Hornettes for whom I had once played. We had many victories, including District and Bi-District championships, and I learned the importance of not just the school's, but the entire town's surrounding a program and being one of its sources of strength. My tenure with the Lockney High School was by far one of the most conducive coaching situations I have ever known, thanks to its school administrators. They believed in me and in what I was trying to do through athletics, and I am eternally grateful for their confidence. After six years of coaching the Lockney Longhorns, I began to feel a nudge toward the next step in my career. I never dreamed that Longhorns of another sort would be on my radar screen.

In all honesty, I did not have a clue about my next step, but I knew it was time to move on. As with any major decision, I prayed that God would put me in the right place. I felt so good about that prayer that I actually resigned my job at Lockney before I had another employment position in place! I'm sure my parents were thrilled about that prospect. I truly thought, through several signals I was getting, that I was supposed to be the next head coach at Angelo State University in San Angelo, Texas, a few hours south of Lubbock. I enthusiastically went through the interview process there fully expecting to get the job, as I had also completed my master's degree in education—plus the fact that I had had such good coaching experience at Lockney. In the end, ASU decided to hire a woman from Michigan, instead of this self-assured West Texas girl. She had a year of college head-coaching experience, which I did not have. I was devastated. I began to doubt myself and began wondering what I was to do with my life.

About a month later, a good friend of mine, Melynn Hunt, called and told me that Jeannine McHaney, the women's athletic director at Texas Tech, had called her looking for an assistant coach. Melynn had given her my name. My heart leaped at the prospect, and I was immediately consumed with fear. How could a little ol' gal from Tulia be ready to coach at such a large university? Jeannine called me, and we went through another interview process. By some miracle, I got the job. For the next several months, I went through an extremely emotional experience. Leaving the wonderful people of Lockney, moving to a community that seemed overwhelmingly large to me, and working at a university which was bigger than any town I had ever lived in appeared to be an insurmountable challenge. Everything about my job intimidated me. The responsibilities, the people, the players, and the head coach, Donna Wick, all combined to make an extremely new and frightening scenario. I really thought many times that I had missed a cue, and that I would never survive this scene!

As with most things, the reality proved to be entirely different. Donna Wick treated me wonderfully, and Jeannine was a terrific leader and mentor. However, there was still an uneasy feeling that overcame me almost daily. I felt uncomfortable, and I certainly missed the environment in Lockney,

Marsha is all smiles after 500 wins.

An Olympic-sized hug from Sheryl Swoopes.

where I had wonderful friends and went about my days brimming with confidence and enthusiasm. I realize now that I was scared and homesick and truly did not feel tall in any sense of the word. As I look back on that year, however, I know that it was all part of a grand plan meant only for me. I needed that year to prove myself and to prepare me for the future. The learning curve was steep, both professionally and personally, but I learned a huge lesson—in order to grow in any area of one's life, a person must get out of his or her comfort zone. I was definitely out of mine that first year as a Red Raider. Unfortunately, the feeling would get worse before it got better.

The following August, after my initial year as assistant coach, Donna Wick resigned rather suddenly to pursue a business career away from Lubbock. Under Coach Wick, the Lady Raiders' win/loss record was 31–29. I was excited for Donna because she had found a great opportunity, but she had left a great opportunity behind. I desperately wanted the head coaching job and began gathering my courage. I was twenty-nine years old and wanted to walk down the hall to visit with Jeannine about my chances. I had to make her think that I had all of the maturity necessary to handle any situation which would arise. I went through everything I wanted to say in front of a mirror a thousand times, in my car as I drove to the gym, and behind the closed door of the tiny ten-by-ten cubicle which was my office. Then one day the phone rang, and Jeannine said she was ready to see me. For the first time in my life, my knees were so weak I did not know if I could walk. When I finally got to the appropriate office and walked in, I just looked at Jeannine and simply said, "Please let me have this job!" All of my valiant talks to the mirror disappeared into a pool of pleading. Jeannine looked at me pitifully for a few moments. Her gruff response to me is one I will treasure all of my life: "Kid, I am going to give you a shot at this, but do not screw it up!" I remember bolting out of my chair, quickly thanking her from the bottom of my heart, promising her I was worthy of her trust, and then sprinting out of the office and down the hall, before she changed her mind.

She and I laughed about that conversation many times through our years together. But that was the beginning of the Lady Raider program as we know it today. Most of what I have accomplished in the field of collegiate athletics is due to Jeannine's initial faith in me. It is highly appropriate then, that I dedicate this book to her, with a promise that I am still trying not to screw it up.

MARSHA SHARP

Autumn 2004

FOREWORD

ONE OF THE HIGHLIGHTS OF MY LIFE WAS REPRESENTING THE USA ON THE 2000 olympic Women's Basketball Team in Sydney, Australia. I have competed in two other Olympics—Atlanta and Athens—both of which were just as glorious, but the 2000 Olympics will always be special because of the people with whom I shared it. Following the presentation of our gold medals, one of the first things I wanted to do was share the moment with the person who helped me get there. My coach, my mentor, and my friend Marsha Sharp had made her way from Lubbock to Sydney to watch me play and to support the USA team. I ran up the bleachers of that arena filled with about 18,000 fans, searching the crowd for my 5' 4" coach. I realized then that I was half-a-world away from Brownfield, Texas, where my passion for women's basketball had begun. When I finally made my way to her, I took off the gold medal I had just been awarded, and placed it around her neck. That was an incredible moment, not unlike the moment seven years earlier when the Lady Raiders won the national championship, and the nation began to know of Texas Tech's incredible basketball program under Coach Sharp's amazing leadership.

Sheryl Swoopes shares her 2000 Olympic gold medal with Coach Sharp in Sydney, Australia.

I can honestly say that Marsha Sharp is the single individual in my life who has had the most influence on me as a person. From the very beginning, she was always about Sheryl Swoopes the person, first, and Sheryl Swoopes the basketball player, second. She makes all of her players realize that someday, playing basketball will be a distant memory for us. The roar of the crowd, the media attention, the endorsements, the echo of *"Swooooooopes"* lingering in the air when I make a shot—all of these, while so satisfying and important, will someday disappear. Coach Sharp always made me understand that what will be left are the relationships I shared with those whose time on earth happened to coincide with mine. One of the opportunities I am most grateful for is to have learned and grown under the leadership of one of the greatest teachers of the game. I have loved basketball for nearly all of my life. Coach Sharp has, too. But, she is the one who taught me that talents are to be used for greater ends than glory or fame. They are a complement to our personal being and are the means we have for making a good difference in the world.

I am honored to write the foreword for this book that explains the wonder of what Coach Sharp's players have always known—leadership with integrity matters, talent without teamwork never wins, dreams are worth going after, and the legacy a person leaves is always more important than any win/loss record.

I will always be grateful to God for blessing me with the great joy of playing basketball and for leading me to the coach who could make me better, not only as a player, but as a person. Former Lady Raider, Carolyn Thompson-Conwright, once said that role models come in all sizes and colors. But because of who she is and what she taught me, Coach Sharp's shadow will always be taller than mine.

SHERYL SWOOPES

August 2004

INTRODUCTION

"O body swayed to music, O brightening glance,
How can we know the dancer from the dance?"
W. B. YEATS, *Among School Children*

IT SEEMS STRANGE TO ME HOW DIFFERENT THE WORLDS OF TWO PRODUCTS OF THE same small town can be. Growing up in Tulia, Texas, one would think that most people would have similar backgrounds and interests, having been exposed to the same high school, the same extracurricular activities, even the same bumps in the road as we traveled down Dip Street on West Texas evenings, circling the monument at the town square, honking at friends. Marsha Sharp and I did those things, albeit a few years apart, and teenagers in Tulia continue to do those things even now. Not much has changed. However, our lives took different directions following our graduation from high school and then, as fate would have it, our paths would intersect again in ways neither of us would have ever dreamed.

Marsha's formative years in Tulia centered around being a banker's daughter, working cattle or pigs on the family farm, excelling in academics, singing in the First Baptist Church Youth Choir, and honing a love for sports, especially basketball. My world centered around being a doctor's daughter, working summers in his office (under the supervision of Marsha's mom, Mary Dell), taking piano lessons, accompanying the First Baptist Church Youth Choir, and honing a love for sports, especially tennis. I knew a bit about basketball and even considered playing at one time because I found myself taller than most of the players on our high school team. However, my tomboy aspirations of game-winning free throws got no farther than the asphalt on our driveway. My youngest sister, however, convinced my parents that she could be a Little Dribbler *and* take piano lessons. Therefore, my earliest experience of being a basketball fan was cheering on the Queens, my sister's team, laughing at all of their missed shots and clumsy ball handling.

It was during the summer before my senior year that I began to take more of an interest in basketball and the Sharp family. Marsha's younger brother, David, was home from college, and his mother thought that he ought to ask me out. All summer I was quite interested in that prospect, but it wasn't until the weekend before David was to return to Baylor that he finally asked me to go to the movies. I guess that left him a good "out," in case our date was something less than perfect. The Tulia Drive-In was showing "Love at First Bite" (no kidding) with George Hamilton, so off we went. That proved to be the beginning of a ten-year courtship. When David asked me to marry him in the fall of 1988, little did I know what I was saying "yes" to. He had always jokingly said that his claim to fame was being Marsha Sharp's brother. I soon came to realize that even being Marsha Sharp's sister-in-law carried some clout around town. While attending basketball games that first season, I began to understand the finer points of NCAA women's basketball. This was a whole new world for me, and I realized that a whole segment of Lubbock's entertainment culture revolved around hoop season. It was *March Madness*. Never before had I seen such enthusiastic fans. I always thought my brother-in-law, Paul, to be a rather soft-spoken sort, but when he started to get after a referee, I just had to turn my head and stare. I learned that as a Lady Raider fan, especially one with the last name of Sharp, one was not to wear any shade of orange at any time. Ever. Period. I learned that if we were going to a game with David's parents, we would be there just after the coliseum lights were turned on and would leave just before they were turned off. I learned that no longer was women's basketball a half-court game, but that it was an exciting brand of strategy, speed, accuracy, and finesse. Countless times during those first seasons, when games would tick down to the final moments and scores were close, David would lean over to me and say, "They're (the other team) about to be out-coached." And sure enough, nine times out of ten, the Lady Raiders would be victorious. That, to me, has always been an amazing thing. I learned, too, that catching *March Madness* is an easy thing to do. When the Lady Raiders played the University of Texas this year, I found myself following our three-point shots to the basket with my arm, as if they needed my help from the stands. When a shot did go in and my beaded Girl-Power bracelet flew off my wrist, beaning a bald-headed fan three rows in front of me, I knew that basketball fever had claimed me, too.

There is, however, little separation between Marsha Sharp, the coach, and Marsha Sharp, the human being. Off the basketball court, the only thing noticeably missing is the fierceness of her competitive spirit. It does, however, make its presence known in the way Marsha constantly encourages those around her. Her dedication is clearly evident to her closest circle of friends who count on her loyalty and unconditional acceptance of who they are. An avid note writer, countless fans and friends in the Lubbock area have been the recipient of one of her letters of thanks or encouragement. Most former players and coaches remain Marsha's friends for life. Her home has been the scene of both bridal and baby showers for her players. That so many of her former students have become successes in their own right is a testimony to Marsha's influence, not to mention her players' 99% graduation rate. When gifted players come her way, it's as if the spark of their giftedness is enhanced in both player and coach. Watching that mutual recognition makes for great basketball entertainment and is an

Nephews Jeremy Martin, Michael Sharp, Jonathan Sharp, and Bradley Martin
accompany Coach Sharp to the Hall of Fame in style.

example of the adage, "When the student is ready, the teacher will appear."

It was during a two-month sojourn when our family lived with Marsha that I realized some of what a coach's life is all about. We were in transition between Denver, Colorado and Lubbock, Texas and lived with her during the summer. When Marsha was home during that time between recruiting season and basketball camp, it was for a two or three day turn around filled with catching up with bills, laundry, family, friends, and fielding phone calls from prospective recruits. I realized that her refrigerator attests to her busy life, as it is filled with large containers of pickles, ketchup, and mustard left over from camp or hamburger cookouts for her players. And that's about all. At family gatherings, Marsha can laughingly be counted on to bring the mustard. The other large commodity in Marsha's home, which speaks of her life, is her collection of coffee cups. One cabinet is stacked three cups high with souvenirs from all over the United States and abroad during her summer stints as the "celebrity" on Ex-Student Association excursions or her many coaching forays, such as coaching the USA Team in Brazil. A testament to her finest achievement so far is the pair of sideline chairs from the 1993 NCAA Championship placed in her game room.

Marsha's encouragement seems to make the most difference with her four nephews. Bradley, Jeremy, Jonathan, and Michael are stars in Marsha's West Texas sky and she is their Auntie Mame, refusing them nothing. She

Coach Sharp and her nephews, Michael and Jonathan, enjoy a moment in Hawaii.

regularly invites them for once in a lifetime experiences, such as flying to one of Michael Jordan's last games or going to Walt Disney World. One of her favorite things to do with our son, Jonathan, is to watch late-night *Zorro* movies or try to play his most recent Nintendo game. Each nephew has received a cool pair of brand new Nikes on more than one occasion. It is to her credit that she takes an interest in *their* interests at every age. In at least two cases, her influence is making a huge difference. Our youngest son, Michael, at age 2, was quite put out when he finally recognized Marsha coaching on the sidelines, and she paid no attention to his shouting "HEY!" and pointing fingers at her from ten rows up. Her face on the TV was one of the first he recognized. But the best story comes from our son, Jonathan, who, after being tucked in bed one night, related to me how one of his classmates was talking about what he wanted to be when he grew up. A few seconds passed, and I asked, "Well, what do you think you want to be, Jonathan?"

"A coach," was his instant reply.

"What kind of coach?" I asked, knowing the answer.

"Basketball," he said without an ounce of hesitation. With that, he sat upright in bed and asked, "Mommy, what does it mean when Aunt Marsha does this on the sideline?" He held up his hand in a clenched fist. I had seen Marsha use the sign many times before but had no clue as to what it might mean. I replied that I wasn't sure, but that I thought it signaled some kind of play.

"We'll have to ask your dad," I lamely contributed.

He lay down and confidently said, "No, it doesn't mean that. It means 'Ya'll come over here. I have another plan.'" If one can do such a thing, I grinned loudly in the dark, praying that he couldn't hear my giggles, and sat there in wonder about Marsha's influence on him and how many basketball games were in all of our futures. I have often thought that in a larger sense as well, there was another plan, a different dream for Marsha to fulfill. As Harley Redin had said, she was "too short and too slow" to be a good player. But he saw in her the potential makings of an excellent coach. He gave her the job of coaching the freshman team, the Queen Bees, during her junior and senior years—a tall order for one whose physical height is all of five-feet-four-inches. She exhibited, however, great knowledge of the game, a passion for winning, and a calling to make a difference for young women through the avenue of sport. Twenty-two years later, she has twice been named National Coach of the Year, become the 22nd NCAA Division I coach to achieve 500 career wins, and has just this spring enjoyed the ribbon cutting ceremony for the Marsha Sharp Center for Student Athletes at Texas Tech University. Her accomplishments cast a tall shadow, then, not only over the West Texas communities she calls home, but also over the lives she has coached for more than two decades.

It is my privilege to help tell Marsha's extraordinary story of coaching and leadership. My journey from being a semi-interested sideline Little Dribbler fan to being an avid Lady Raider fan is a story of being seduced. I have been wooed by the artistry of the game, the finesse of the player's athleticism, the intensity of focus by both players and coaches, the desire of many of her players to use their giftedness to further their education and thus, their station in life, the thrill of winning, and, yes, the roar of the crowd. All of that would be nothing, however, without the passionate class-act of Coach Sharp, the short gal from Tulia who orchestrates it all—from coordinating plays, to igniting fans, to venting her opinions with the referees, to inspiring players to reach deep within themselves to use their God-given abilities—she is the hub around which it all turns. Watching how all aspects of the game radiate from her skills is truly a thing of beauty. Even if I hadn't grown up in the same town and married her brother, I would still be one of her greatest fans and mad about Marsha. How can we know the dancer from the dance?

EMILY FOREMAN SHARP

Spring 2004

*a portion of this Introduction appeared as an article in the March 2000 issue of Lubbock Magazine *under the title, "Reflections from an Unlikely Fan"*

Coach Sharp shares a Hall of Fame moment with co-author, Emily F. Sharp.

VISION

1982–1983
Lady Raider Average Home Game Attendance: 876

Give to us clear vision that we may know where to stand and what to stand for—because unless we stand for something, we shall fall for anything."

REV. PETER MARSHALL
Senate chaplain offered at the opening of the session, April 18, 1947

EANNINE MCHANEY WAS THE WOMEN'S ATHLETIC Director at Texas Tech in 1982, the year she hired me, a twenty-nine-year-old rookie, as the university's head coach for women's basketball. Jeannine had as much vision and saw the big picture as well as anyone I have ever been associated with. Therefore, it was no surprise that first fall when she asked me to list my long-term goals for Lady Raider Basketball and, more importantly, the steps required to get there. I did that, and then she and I, with my new assistant coach, Linden Weese, sat down and discussed each goal in detail. These included, in no particular order, the following list: graduating players, winning a conference title, consistently appearing in the top-twenty nationally-ranked teams, selling out the Lubbock Coliseum, and winning a national championship.

I remember the three of us talking very seriously about all of those challenges and what it would take to overcome them. We talked at length about budget, recruitment, support staff, facilities, fan support, and other ingredients that we thought would be necessary steps toward our goals. We also talked about the fact that this would be a very long process and that many of the steps would have to be taken one at a time. Still, we had a plan.

I was obviously extremely excited about my new position and about the vision I had for the future of women's basketball at Texas Tech. My first impulse was to talk about it with people—people in the athletic department, community people, friends, family, and anyone else who would listen. I remember getting my feelings hurt on many occasions when people would laugh when I told them our plan, or even worse, when I felt like they were patronizing me. When I look back on it now, I guess the reality that we were playing in front of about 200 people a game and had not come even close to winning a conference championship, much less being in the top twenty, made our goals sound a little out of reach. However, after having been through the process, I have some sense of what had to happen to make these seemingly impossible dreams a reality.

First of all, at the beginning of any great endeavor, it is important to realize the difference between long-term and short-term success. There is a huge

The Lady Raider locker room floor.

difference in building a great program and having a great year. I know lots of coaches and people in other professions who want instant success that would lead them to something else. Many of these have been impatient dreamers and would compromise basic principles to achieve short-lived greatness. You know these kinds of folks, I'm sure—those who one day are an amazing success and the next day are nowhere to be found. I am a believer that there are very rarely any shortcuts to lasting success.

The same is true in a variety of situations in everyday life. Relationships, for instance, take renewed commitment every day; they should never be taken for granted. If a person wants to become financially secure through investments, one must have a long-term vision that gradually achieves monetary security. The axiom, "If it's too good to be true, it probably is" resonates throughout all of human experience. The dreams we dare to dream take constant commitment, focus, and resolve—every day—from the locker room, to the boardroom, to the family room. Only then will the success we seek be lasting.

There are a number of points for a leader to consider at the beginning of every successful project. First of all, it is important to set goals. What is it that you really want to accomplish? What would be the best outcome of all if you could create it? Again, it is almost impossible to be successful if you do not have a plan. Sometimes people make the mistake of thinking too small or, at the other end of the spectrum, are unrealistic about the future. For instance, at

Roger Reding, Lance White, Marsha Sharp, Melinda Pharies, and Linden Weese
at the Women's Basketball Hall of Fame Induction

some point, it must become apparent that every female basketball player will not be the next Sheryl Swoopes. I do believe, however, that most people do not have enough confidence to pursue their ultimate dreams. Don't let that happen to you. Dream big from the beginning.

Once you have decided on your ultimate goal, make sure you are in the right setting to achieve it. You need to be a "good fit" for your surroundings. For instance, as I said earlier, I am a West Texas person. Texas Tech and the city of Lubbock, Texas, are a good fit for me. I know every back road and every small town throughout most of the state of Texas, but particularly above the Caprock. That has been a major factor in my ability to relate to a large number of our recruits who grew up in towns much like Tulia, Texas (pop. 5148), my hometown. These are small communities with one bricked main street where all the kids hang out, and there is not much else to do but go to the gym and play ball. I understand that culture. It has been a huge part of the success we have enjoyed at Texas Tech. In 1993, when we won the National Championship, all but one of our players were from the state of Texas, and they came from towns such as Nazareth (pop. 356), Brownfield (pop. 9218), Spearman (pop. 2937), and Loraine (pop. 660). You get the picture.

No matter what career path you follow, once you find the situation you are looking for, make sure that as soon as possible you surround yourself with the people, the staff, and the elements you believe will be important in your quest for success. The people you choose to be on your staff will be one of the most important decisions you will ever make. These people need to be folks who share your vision, who have uncompromising loyalty, and who have a great work ethic. And, it will take people with these traits for you to have a chance to accomplish great things. I have been very, very fortunate in the area of staff. Linden Weese has been with me every year that I have been a head coach at Tech. Due to his incredible loyalty and mutual desire for success, we have forged a proven partnership that is a privilege we enjoy every day. The Lady Raider program could never have achieved what it has without his help, his humor, and his unforgettable presence.

Roger Reding joined our staff in 1990 and has shared the same kind of vision, loyalty, and dedication. He brought many personal gifts to our program which have helped us to win, but one of the most important is his ability to connect us with junior college players. Sheryl Swoopes was the first example, but great players such as Angie Braziel, Aleah Johnson, Connie Robinson, Tabitha Truesdale, and Candi White are examples of the experienced players he has recruited to Tech. He has been a very important piece of the puzzle, and I appreciate the commitment he brings us every day.

Lance White joined our staff in 1992 as a student assistant. He called the office one day and asked if he could just hang around and watch how we work. He said he would do anything we needed—wash towels, sweep the floors—anything just to be there. I have probably never been around anyone with as much energy, as good a work ethic, or as many creative ideas as Lance. I could never begin to tell you everything he did for us on a daily basis or how many ways he helped make my job a little more manageable. Every once in a while, you are blessed to be around a person who sees things to do and just does them without anyone asking or even anyone knowing. That is a special talent in itself, and it is wonderful for a program to have someone like that. After eleven years with the Lady Raiders, Lance is now pursuing his own vision as an assistant coach in Florida. I look forward to the special contributions he will make to women's basketball and will always be thankful for his friendship and assistance.

Krista Kirkland Gerlich joined our staff as an assistant coach in 2003. Her story is told later in the book, but it is especially gratifying to me when someone who has gone through our program, then makes the choice to continue the vision by choosing coaching as a profession. Many of our former players are now coaches themselves, dedicated to visions of their own and making positive differences in the lives of young people. Krista does that on a daily basis for us, and I am blessed to have her on our team again.

A DIFFERENT KIND OF VISION

Carolyn Thompson-Conwright

FORWARD

1980-1984

Hobbs, New Mexico

THE HALLS OF ESTACADO HIGH SCHOOL IN Lubbock, Texas, have been graced with many notable personalities, not the least of whom was one of West Texas' greatest athletes and most gifted educators. Former Texas Tech Lady Raider Carolyn Thompson-Conwright not only coached the Estacado Lady Matador basketball team for ten years, but then served as the school's principal. Her office was the home of the woman in charge, a leader who cast a tall shadow, not only in terms of physical presence, but also in terms of attitude, achievement, and aspiration. Estacado students didn't even think of coming to her office with anything pierced but ears—much less sporting a bad attitude. And they learned that the only place for a comb is in your pocket or purse, not jauntily placed in your hair in an attempt to be cool. Her tenure as

principal honed her natural leadership skills and prepared her for her current position as an administrator with the Lubbock Independent School District. A three-time college basketball All-American, Mrs. Thompson-Conwright knows what it takes for students to succeed and possesses one of those rare personalities which exudes authority. She also believes she has a long-term calling in education and enjoys the opportunity to help young people dream big dreams. Upon reflection, however, Thompson-Conwright agrees that it wasn't always that way.

When she appeared on the campus of Texas Tech University in 1980, she thought she was going to be on the volleyball team. That was why she was recruited, and that was the education ticket she rode all the way from Hobbs, New Mexico. However, when she got to Lubbock, she looked around and thought she'd have much more fun playing basketball. She knew more girls on the team and liked woman who was the girls' basketball coach at that time, Donna Wick. So, somehow, she found herself playing basketball. That was cool with her. It was going to be fun either way, and that was what she wanted college to be—fun. However, at the beginning of her sophomore season, she ran up against Coach Wick's new assistant coach, Marsha Sharp, whom she decided she was not going to like. What did this "little short white lady" think she could teach her about life? What was she, 5'2"? Okay, 5'4". Here this coach was, fresh out of "perfy-poo" Wayland Baptist, always talking and philosophizing about basketball when all Thompson-Conwright wanted to do was play.

"Always talking, always more into

Carolyn Thompson shoots a jumper against Texas.

Carolyn Thompson's jersey retirement ceremony—January 3, 1985.

the mental thing, always organized and making plans to win. I didn't want any part of that," she laughs. They bumped heads for a while; Coach Sharp didn't think the players, especially Thompson-Conwright, should be given as much leeway as they were given. Also, most of the girls Thompson had looked forward to playing with had left because of the coaching change; she didn't even get a chance to play with them with the exception of Reina Cherry. Reina is her good friend now, but one day she gave Thompson-Conwright a tour of Lubbock she would never forget—Reina took the rookie around and showed her where all the churches were. "I thought 'man, this is not my idea of fun in college.'" They still laugh together about that. Thompson-Conwright recalls, "What kept aggravating me about Coach Sharp was that she kept acknowledg-

ing my personal being rather than my being an athlete. She kept giving us a vision of ourselves after basketball and wanted to know how the non-athletic part of our lives was going. And that's how she won me. She kept asking what my vision was of myself."

The basketball part of Carolyn's life went relatively smoothly. She recalls thinking that playing basketball well was her reason for being there. She was a competitor, a playmaker who continues even today to believe that if a person is going to do a thing, she should give it her all. And that's what she did. She was named Most Valuable Player all four years while accumulating the most points earned in a basketball career at Texas Tech—men's or women's basketball—with a 2,655 point-record that still stands. Ironically, she does not believe she is an overachiever.

Thompson-Conwright handles her career and family life with a healthy balance; she and her husband James work as a team to care for all the needs of their three-year-old son Blair, just as her LISD administrative team handles any crisis at work. She wants Blair to know about his mother's athletic accomplishments and will tell him the stories of her basketball career when he is ready.

And there are plenty of stories. Carolyn remembers playing when the echo of her voice would bounce off the empty seats of the Lubbock Coliseum. She didn't think about it in a negative way, though. "We used to bribe our roommates and friends to come yell and watch us play. We usually had very few fans unless we played before a men's game. It was so great, though, because any time you wanted to find a person in the stands, you could just look up and find them. Now it'd be pretty hard to do given the size of the United Spirit Arena."

As far as building a team was concerned, Carolyn's assessment was that they weren't as talented as everyone thought they were. She reflects, "After Coach Wick left, Coach Sharp probably inherited material she would have never recruited, but she made us believe in her. It just happened, kind of like magic, that we made more out of ourselves than was actually there. Coach Sharp gave us a bigger vision. She said we were going to fly to games in planes instead of drive in buses. She made things happen that we had never even thought of happening."

The highest moment in Thompson-Conwright's basketball career came when her jersey was retired. It was January 3, 1985, and in the middle of Coach Sharp's third season as head coach. The former Lady Raider MVP knew it was going to occur before Tech played the University of Texas. It was cold outside, and she mused, "You know, I don't think I'll even go. Why do they want to retire my jersey anyway? I think it's got sweat rings on it!" She admits, however, that it was Coach Sharp's idea to retire it as a way of thanking Thompson-Conwright for what she gave the Lady Raider program, as well as to tell folks that this was a visionary step. Her retired jersey, number 44, hangs today in Lubbock's United Spirit Arena beside just two others—Krista Kirkland Gerlich's number 21 and Sheryl Swoopes' number 22. Thompson-Conwright reflects, "Coach Sharp wanted to put women's basketball on the map at Texas Tech. She was really smart about it. I think retiring my jersey was one way of saying 'This is just the beginning. Just watch and see where we're going.'"

Coach Thompson oversees Estacado High School standout Patrice Conwright signing her Lady Raider letter of intent.

Obviously, I have been so very fortunate to surround myself with quality people like these who are loyal, who share my vision, and who have the work ethic it takes to be successful. Assembling a staff like this is a critical part of good leadership, good coaching, and central to the success of the Lady Raider program.

Once you've surrounded yourself with the right staff, the support of the organization that employs you is integral for long-term success in achieving your vision. There is no question, for instance, that the universities that made a commitment to develop and promote women's athletics in the early 1970s really separated themselves from the pack and continue to hold an edge today. The administrative support for that vision is crucial on many fronts. First of all, these are the people who control the purse strings—they make decisions on a daily basis about how funds are allocated. In the case of athletics, the administration's philosophy about supporting broad-based athletic programs will definitely play a major role in a coach's ability to be successful. Unfortunately, the reverse is also true: they could make decisions to support only a small segment of a department, thereby limiting the success of your program. I have been fortunate to work for numerous administrators at Texas Tech who believed in Title IX and afforded opportunities to women athletes, not only because it was the law, but more importantly, because they believed it was the right thing to do. Believe me, it can make a world of difference.

Secondly, your administration also controls other logistical aspects of the program. Successful athletic programs are heavily dependent on coordinating game schedules, workout sessions, and facility access. For instance, what times during the day will your team be able to workout? I have heard many horror stories from my colleagues who would have to workout at night or maybe at 6:00AM just because their male counterparts wanted to reserve the facility all afternoon—just in case it was needed! Your administrative boss should be your advocate concerning all aspects of your training, recruitment, travel, and equipment. In short, he or she must share your vision and the proof of it is in the way the details are handled.

Third, as a leader, you need administrative support that can connect you with the 'movers and shakers' who also support your vision. You know, these are the folks who can make the contributions, fund the scholarships, and fill up the stands for your games. If your relationship with your administration is weak, it is much harder to create these ties with the boosters who can take you to another level. Some of my best moments have been after big wins, when I have been able to share those successes with my bosses and benefactors. Because of my sheer respect for them, I wanted our program's success to be a satisfying reward for their faith in us.

So, now you've pinpointed your vision, assembled a like-minded staff, and garnered the support of your administration. What next? Transfer all of these positives into a day-to-day plan that generates results! It is sometimes a tedious process to set short-term goals in order to execute a plan. There are no short cuts here—this is just plain hard work. It's getting down in the trenches and getting dirty. Let me give you some coaching examples: putting together workout schedules, getting your staff on the same page with objectives for each practice, executing that practice, evaluating that practice, and starting all over the next day. That may not seem very difficult at first glance, but consider that you must add in the diverse personalities of up to fifteen players, the stress of getting game-ready, trying to cover as many weaknesses as possible, and playing to as many strengths as possible. Add in the fact that on a daily basis you will be dealing with many office distractions which range from recruiting, public relations, media, budgets, travel schedules, camp preparations, and public appearances and...you get the picture. All leaders find themselves in this sort of multi-tasking nightmare. Learning to navigate through them is essential to achieving your vision.

Throughout my career with the Lady Raider program, five coping strategies have been invaluable in tackling our day-to-day demands: Delegation, Focus, Consistency, Flexibility, and Non-Negotiables. Whether building a team, running a business, or organizing a family, relying on these five simple tools makes realizing big dreams possible.

DELEGATION

THE DEGREE TO WHICH I FOLLOW THE DISCIPLINE OF DELEGATION IS ONE OF THE crucial keys to the success of our program. These day-to-day tasks must be given to the persons most equipped to complete them, and it is important to add that there is always more than one way to tackle a task. After you delegate a job, then you must trust the staff person to get it done in the way most familiar to him or her. You will have to bite your tongue every once in a while because you might have a different way of handling an assignment, but you will surely build trust and confidence in your staff if you will let them fly.

While the doing of even the most menial task is important, there are some jobs which only the head coach can address. For example, I could come to work every day and stay extremely busy and really accomplish tasks that, in one sense, are very important. I could wash towels, sweep the gym floor, clean the locker room, and stuff recruiting mail. I would have worked hard

and, believe me, I am not above doing any one of these tasks. However, I must be efficient at delegating some of these tasks to capable staff members, so that I can tackle other areas such as getting administrative support, connecting with fans, dealing with media or studying film. There is plenty of work to go around, but I was hired to *lead*—delegation is a must!

FOCUS

FOCUS IS CRITICAL TO THE ACCOMPLISHMENT OF ANY GOAL. AS A COACH, PROBABLY the best example, and the one that is the biggest challenge for me, is to leave everything else in the office when I go to practice. No matter what recruit just told me "no," no matter what speaking engagement I have later, or what goofy question a media person just asked me, I have to leave it and focus on the day's task. Isn't that what I ask of my players? Isn't that what managers ask of their employees? Give the task at hand your undivided attention; it will be critical to your success. This is a learned skill. It will help you to be able to sit down and take care of pending tasks one at a time in an efficient manner. Otherwise, a disorganized mound of work will overwhelm you. Then frustration sets in, and it is even more difficult to operate. The failure to focus one's energies has caused many a potential leader to drop out of sight. Don't let lack of focus be your downfall.

Every part of your vision should be analyzed and broken down into a daily plan. Some individuals call these task grids, a term I think is extremely appropriate. The more detailed these plans can be, the more productive a staff will be. It also gives you the opportunity to see if one staff member is overloaded, while another may not be involved enough. You should put a great deal of thought and time into developing this daily agenda. I can tell you that your staff will be much happier if they have clear expectations and a focused plan with which to implement them.

CONSISTENCY

UNFORTUNATELY, IT WILL BE NATURAL TO LET LITTLE THINGS SLIP FROM TIME TO time because of the simple monotony of daily tasks. However, your consistency at staying on task will be a huge factor in your success. Think for a minute about how committed coaches are about repetitions in practice to insure that players are fundamentally sound. The same is true for the daily operation of any program. Inconsistency causes confusion and makes it extremely difficult to have good productivity. Lady Raider players understand that when they

The Texas Tech Court Jesters fire up the crowd.

show up for practice, they should be consistently ready to work. Likewise, I understand that I must be consistently ready to coach and have ready a workout plan that makes the most of our time together. I am not simply talking about being consistent for a month or a year, but for several decades in order to build a vision that you will really be proud to claim.

FLEXIBILITY

WHILE CONSISTENCY IS CRUCIAL, I MUST AT LEAST ALSO SAY THAT A CERTAIN AMOUNT of flexibility is necessary. If there is something in your system that is not working, don't be afraid to change it. Individuals who are afraid of change will not survive. If there is a more effective way to do business, to coach three-pointers, to communicate, or to provide for your family, you must have enough confidence in yourself to make the change. For example, when I first began coaching I was fairly rigid about adhering to fundamental skills of playing basketball, specifically about various types of defensive and offensive plays. However, when recruits come to the Lady Raider program from other parts of the country, where they have been taught different methods, I've learned that sometimes it is better to allow players to play with the skills they know best rather than trying to force a new skill on them that achieves the same result. The old story about the daughter who cooks the roast the same way for years, just like her mother did, illustrates the point. The mother consistently cut the ends off the roast before cooking it, every time without fail; the daughter thought that technique was her mother's secret to a perfect roast, but when the old matriarch was asked why she did so, she replied, "Well, back in those days, that was the only way the roast would fit in my small pan." Some of your methods of operation might need examining to see if they are really right for what you are trying to do. Never be afraid to change.

NON-NEGOTIABLES

IT IS ALWAYS IMPORTANT AT THE BEGINNING OF ANY ENTERPRISE TO DETERMINE the values which will not be compromised. I call this drawing a line in the sand or pinpointing the things not up for discussion—in short, the "non-negotiables." These values are never flexible, are always consistent, and are always necessary in order to navigate through the gray areas of leadership which will inevitably come. That these non-negotiables might be different for you and me is not the point; it is just very important that we are true to ourselves. We are all put in situations where our non-negotiables will be tested. This is back to the "short-cut mentality" of success we mentioned earlier. Flash-in-the-pan success stories always seem to compromise some-

"NICE TO MEET YOU. WILL YOU COACH MY TEAM?"

MELYNN HUNT HAS KNOWN COACH SHARP FOR TWENTY YEARS, BUT THE MOST vivid memory she has is the first time the two met. Hunt was a rookie high school coach completing her first varsity job at Lubbock-Cooper High School when Sharp was coaching at Lockney, Texas. The two had entered their junior varsity teams in a tournament in Slaton, Texas. Coach Hunt was seated in the stands with her team watching Sharp coach the Lockney Longhorns in the game preceding Lubbock-Cooper's. Hunt remembers that the officiating in the game had been slightly less than horrible, and that the Lady Longhorns weren't playing so well. Coach Sharp was not happy. Hunt looked up from taping one of her player's ankles and saw four of Sharp's substitute players retreating down the sideline, having been duly admonished by their diminutive coach. Sharp then turned her back to the playing floor and began to kick the heck out of the bench. One of the officials gave the frustrated coach a technical foul and things quickly went from bad to worse. In those days, coaches weren't ejected from a game until after the third technical foul. Coach Sharp got two "T's" and then called a time out. She walked across the floor to a wide-eyed Coach Hunt and said, very calmly, "If I get one more, you are going to have to coach my team." And that was how Melynn Hunt met Marsha Sharp. Hunt nodded her head "yes" and began to pray that Sharp didn't pick up that third "T." She didn't, but that exchange began a friendship that has lasted twenty years.

where on values. I know this for a fact: Long-term projects that produce the most satisfying rewards are always built around the philosophy that values are not for sale. Consider which values you will not negotiate and stick with them. You will always be glad you did.

Over twenty years of pursuing my vision has taught me volumes about delegation, focus, consistency, flexibility, and values. While I'm sure I've made mistakes along the way, I do know this: Any worthwhile vision must begin with what you want to accomplish, not only at the end of the day, but at the end of your career. It encompasses the discipline of setting both long-term and short-term goals, as well as an uncompromising adherence to values you deem important. Then, armed with vision, balanced by values, spurred by your unique talents, and undergirded by faith, you can boldly take the first steps of a fascinating and rewarding journey meant only for you.

RECRUITING

1985–1986
Lady Raider Average Home Game Attendance: 1044

People of talent resemble a musical instrument
more closely than they do a musician.
Without outside help, they produce not a single sound,
but given even the slightest touch,
and a magnificent tune emanates from them.
FRANZ GRILLPARZER, *Notebooks and Diaries, (1811-1816)*

HAVE ALWAYS BELIEVED THAT RECRUITING THE RIGHT INDI-
viduals for a team or organization was the most important
step to ensure success. If people are not the right "fit,"
the group will never reach its full potential. First of all,
there is no question that any organization must have
the talent to be great. There is no way a team can be successful without innate talent. A team can't survive,
much less expect to reach great heights, without it. It is
very important that a coach be able to evaluate possible
recruits and make educated decisions about the natural
giftedness of each potential player. A player should
never be expected to find talent after he or she shows
up in an organization. That is just not going to happen. If a Clydesdale is
recruited, that player is not going to turn into a racehorse regardless of the
coach. There may be a place for a powerful Clydesdale in the program, but a
coach should never expect that person to perform differently after he or she
arrives. Recruiting expectations, then, must be realistic.

However, the factors imperative in determining your key players—the
ones who are most likely to boost your organization to greatness—are
probably the hardest to define, and, in some cases, the hardest to discover.
This challenge forces coaches and leaders to earn their pay, work their
hardest, and probably separate themselves from the pack. I call it determining the intangibles. Honestly, it is easy to walk into a gym and within several
minutes, find players who are talented enough to play Division I basketball.
However, to ascertain if they have the intangibles necessary to fit into an
existing team might take several years of study. Potential basketball recruits
must be watched in as many situations as possible, our coaches must research
them with as many people who know them as possible, and the entire organization must get to know them as well as possible within the recruiting rules.

It is also important to remember that just because a player might be a
good fit for Lady Raider Basketball doesn't mean she would be a good fit
somewhere else. Some personal qualities are more important for one coach
than another. That doesn't mean that one perspective is right and the other

Erin Grant takes control of the offense.

RECRUITING PEOPLE AND PLAYERS

Michelle Thomas

GUARD

1992–1996

San Antonio, Texas

WHEN SHE WAS IN HIGH SCHOOL, MICHELLE Thomas remembers a conversation with her father that went something like this, "This little orange ball is your ticket to a better life." Now, Michelle knows her dad was right, but she never dreamed that her ticket's destination would be Texas Tech University. Michelle is a big city girl from Roosevelt High School in San Antonio. "I am not a West Texas gal. This is not where I would like to live the rest of my life, but basketball was my ticket to what I wanted to do with my life. Basketball was my means to my dream." She remembers a pivotal moment in her recruiting process when she knew Texas Tech was the place for her. "Most coaches during recruiting will initially take you to visit the gym or take you on a tour of the locker room. Not at Texas Tech. The first place the coaches took me when I got off the plane was to the law school because

they knew I wanted to be an attorney. My biggest concern had been 'if basketball is taken away from me for some reason, then what?' A 99% graduation rate for players? You don't think that made a difference in my decision to come here?"

If anyone is a passionate poster child for the Lady Raider program, it is Michelle Thomas. "Now, you've got to admit, taking directions from a short, little white lady trying to be hip-hop was a little difficult at first. Why should I listen to somebody who calls a sunroof a 'moon roof'? I learned, though, that this woman knows her x's and o's and is able to deal with any condition. Coach Sharp has built a legacy of consistency. She is classy, she is intelligent, she is the entire package. And, she has built this program from the bottom to the top, all without breaking the rules."

Michelle knows about being at the pinnacle with Coach Sharp as a member of the 1993 National Championship Team. In January 2003, when the players gathered for a reunion to celebrate that "one shining moment," Thomas was the first to speak. "At 3:37 EST ten years ago, we were the best in the country. This is a moment in time to celebrate, a rarity. Not often does something come around that is that pure, that honest, that sincere." She believes that those moments, though, are stepping-stones to building bigger dreams.

Through Michelle's study of criminal defense, she wants to become a representative for the underdogs in the larger community. "When I settle down, I want to make a difference in the community in which I find myself. I want to change something; I want to contribute to righting the injustices of the world."

Michelle Thomas always brought passion to the court.

is wrong. It's just that coaches look for different qualities. The right circumstances are as important for the athlete as for the coach. A player will never accomplish all that she should if the fit is not there.

So, what are the intangibles I look for in potential Lady Raiders? Successful coaches and leaders must have a strong grasp of the principles and ideals that they believe separate the average from the great. These are qualities that I don't compromise and which define my relationship with a player. All coaches have these lines, but invariably, they are different for every individual. The success of the player-coach relationship to a large extent relies on how closely the two share the same values. Of course, exceptions abound, but as a general rule, most greatness is achieved through some combination of these intangibles.

My list is something I have come to call POWER—an acronym representing five qualities that are invaluable to success.

P = PASSION

VERY RARELY IN MY CAREER HAVE I SEEN AN INDIVIDUAL ACHIEVE AT A HIGH LEVEL if he/she is not passionate about the sport. Without this driving love of the game, a player will never have the stamina to compete at the game's highest stage of competition. Erin Grant, freshman starting point guard for the 2002-2003 team and AAU All-American, is a player who brings this kind of passion to the game. While she is not an overachiever by any stretch, she is passionate about the game of basketball. This former Mansfield High School homecoming queen loves the energy of the court and the position of point guard as director of offense for her team. She states, "I like being a leader and kind of come by it naturally." When asked about passionate players who have impacted her career, Grant doesn't hesitate: "Sheryl Swoopes. I just love her game." Erin's dream is to become a WNBA player and she admits that the best thing about being a Lady Raider is "going out to play in the best arena in the country with the best fans in the world." It's that kind of passion to play and win that became so obvious during our recruiting of Erin Grant. It is also that passion for which she received the Fighting Heart Award at the end of the 2003–2004 season. The passion she brings to the basketball court, combined with her innate talent, are two intangible ingredients for greatness. Examine any great leader in any field, and you will find a passion that fuels his or her success.

O = OVERACHIEVER

I HAVE A CONFESSION TO MAKE HERE. PROBABLY THE CHALLENGE IN MY WORLD of coaching is the task of dealing with an underachiever. I avoid that

Celebration in the Lubbock Coliseum.

inevitable conflict if at all possible. The years when I have coached players who fit that description were by far the most miserable of my life and taught me not to compromise this essential standard. I have never understood why anyone would not want to become as great as possible. For me, it is not just always about winning (although I hate to lose), but it is always about trying to be better than your talent and better than the expectations of others. None of us has reached his or her full potential; we are all growing, or should be, and an overachiever simply recognizes that fact and tries to do something about it. Keitha Dickerson is a great example of an overachiever who played for the Lady Raiders from 1996–2000. Her competitive, over-achieving attitude made her a player I could count on in the heat of competition; she would not give up until the final buzzer sounded. Keitha was also a fan favorite because of her passion for winning. Her determination was crucial to our team's getting to the *Elite Eight* in 2000. Every team needs a Keitha who can be counted on for inspiration and example, especially in the tough moments. Honestly, I know I am driven, and I sometimes set my expectations too high, but I still believe that most of us who do not reach our potential simply do not aim high enough. Every coach has the unique opportunity to assemble a "dream team" in every sense of the phrase. Make sure that your team has at least one player who will never give up on his or her dreams.

W = WORK ETHIC

THERE IS NO SUBSTITUTE FOR HARD WORK. NO ONE EVER FULLY BENEFITS FROM any experience without having had to sacrifice to achieve the goal. If there isn't any sweat involved, the goal probably wasn't high enough. Obviously, there are instances where exceptionally talented athletes are able to win without working very hard. For instance, a truly great player might be able to win championships at the high school level just because she is more gifted than her peers. She might even be able to succeed as a freshman, but there will come a point where she cannot survive on talent alone. At that point, it is always interesting to see if she has the inner strength to develop a work ethic when she has never been forced to do so before. Obviously, the ultimate find in recruiting is to discover an individual who not only has great talent, but also knows how to work. Unfortunately, these folks are few and far between!

When I think of an example of a player who possessed incredible work ethic, I immediately think of Jennifer Buck. She played in our program from 1988–1992. She came from an outstanding program at Conroe High School in Texas and came to us with wonderfully high expectations. As many freshmen do, she had a difficult time making the transition from the high school game to Division I basketball. It became more and more apparent early in the season that she was becoming increasingly frustrated, until one day, she had a virtual "melt down." I walked into our training room, and Jennifer was sitting on a table crying uncontrollably. Through her tears she began to tell me how horrible she was, how slow she was, and that she did not think she could ever contribute to the team. I was also in tears because I hurt so for her. At that point, I remember saying that we just had to find a way to fix it, that we would not quit until we got her to a level where she felt successful. In the off-season that followed, I felt fortunate to witness a remarkable transformation I will never forget. Jennifer committed herself to basketball that summer. She worked out in the weight room, jumped rope non-stop, and ran sprints aggressively in an un-air-conditioned workout facility until she was completely spent and drenched. This routine didn't happen every once in a while—it took place daily.

The fact that Jennifer's story has a great ending makes it even more special. She was a starter for us and a major part of both our first conference championship and our conference tournament championship team. She made a huge three-point play in the conference tournament, which helped

An unlucky opponent tries to guard Lady Raider Jennifer Buck.

RECRUITING PEOPLE AND PLAYERS

Melinda Schmucker Pharies

POINT GUARD

1997–2000

Nazareth, Texas

MELINDA SCHMUCKER PHARIES GREW UP IN Nazareth, Texas, a German community just west of Tulia and not far from Coach Sharp's family farm. When Melinda was recruited, she felt like she was being pursued by someone who really knew her, knew small town life and whose family background was similar to her own. She said she always kept her basketball options open, but knew that she would, in the end, be a Lady Raider. Coach Sharp showed Melinda her own best gift—leadership. "In high school, it was easier to get it all done. I played every position—from post, to wing, to high point shooter, to point guard. Coach Sharp recognized that I could really play point guard the best. She never gave up on me and showed me what I could do."

Pharies has a perfect memory of

that. "When we were playing, there were not many of us who could really shoot the ball well, not many who could score. When we were playing Notre Dame in the 2000 *Sweet Sixteen* game in Tennessee, we were down 17 points. Coach Sharp called a time out, huddled us up, and said 'Keep on playing defense. Keep on playing defense.' We were all looking at the score and wanting to say to her, 'Coach, look at the score.' But we went back out and concentrated on what we did best. In the next ten minutes, we scored 17 points and suddenly we were tied. It was like she knew we had it in us and believed that we could do it. We ended up winning that game." Melinda believes that kind of coaching made a huge difference for that game. "Everyone began to believe her," she says.

Melinda completed her playing career as one of Tech's all-time best point guards and still holds the record for assists with 603. Following graduation, Pharies was recruited again by Tech to become assistant director of basketball operations for the Lady Raider team. "What is so great about working here is that I'm helping to build something that Coach Sharp has already been building for twenty years. When I was a player, I was clueless about everything involved. Now I see that basketball is really the smallest part of the whole operation. I see how it all works and how hard everyone must work every day to continue this success." Pharies says that the main job is to make sure everyone—assistants, players, fans, recruits, opponents, media—believes in the program's goals. She believes that vision comes from Coach Sharp's passion for respect in all things.

Melinda Schmucker-Pharies holds the record for assists with 603.

Jolee Ayers and Natalie Ritchie's cheering section.

us win late in the game. One of my favorite memories in coaching took place when that game was decided, and Jennifer lifted me off the ground in a huge hug. This time we were crying together for a different reason. Jennifer Buck has always been proof to me that the intangible quality of a player's work ethic is essential in the development of talent.

E= ENTHUSIASM

IN MY ESTIMATION, ENTHUSIASM IS ESSENTIAL TO THE PSYCHE OF ANY SUCCESSFUL organization. I am amazed at how adding an enthusiastic person to the mix can change the entire atmosphere of the program. There have been years when the whole dynamic of the team has changed by adding the enthusiasm of only one or two new players. I am also always impressed when the whole-hearted contagion of an exciting team on the court spreads to ten thousand people in the stands.

One of the most spirited players I've ever coached is La Toya Davis. She can really ignite a crowd when she pumps her fist after a making a great shot and then is the first player to run down to the other end of the court. I must add, however, that the reverse is also true. If a team is not eager it will find itself playing in front of smaller crowds as the year advances. People are drawn to energy and are not interested in watching athletes who appear simply to be going through the motions. To find out how genuinely enthusiastic a recruit is, I have found it's important to let her have time alone with the other players on our team. Together, the team can discover nuances about their own chemistry that a coach might never find out in an interviewing process. This knowledge is crucial information that could become important down the road. Recruits can put on a show for us, and allowing the team to help discern the intangibles has become an important tool for the Lady Raiders.

R= RESPECT

RESPECT MAY BE THE MOST ALL-ENCOMPASSING QUALITY OF THE INTANGIBLES I would like to see in a recruit. Respect is also the most difficult factor to evaluate within a short period of time. This character trait reveals, first, how a player feels about herself, and second, how much worth a player sees in the people around her. It also reveals if she shares our program's values and whether she can honestly share our vision. I tell our players all the time that a person can't really respect others until she has a sound respect for herself. We also talk about the fact that in a team setting, respecting someone is much more important than liking someone. Often in life we must tolerate an individual we may not like in order to reach a common goal, but we must always respect the talent and commitment of others with whom we share the road. Self-respect is the foundation of personal standards that should never be compromised, and it remains the hallmark of a person's life. People of all ages, but particularly young people, compromise so much of what they believe, making it hard for them to maintain even a minimal level of self-respect. Without self-respect, we don't have the confidence to attempt greatness.

For example, athletes who have a great deal of self-respect overcome adversity and show more courage when confronted with challenges than those who struggle with self-respect. Certainly, when a player brings self-respect to the table it is much easier to share a level of mutual respect with coaches and teammates. This essential intangible greatly increases the chance not only for personal success, but for the success of the team as well.

It is very unrealistic to expect to find the total POWER package in every single player during the recruiting process. The key is to find individuals who have as many of these qualities as possible to match the expectations of others in your organization—not just the players, but the coaching staff as well. Certainly, some of these qualities can be learned and some of them just appear throughout the team building process.

Melinda Schmucker Pharies is a good example of this phenomenon. Growing up playing basketball in Nazareth, Texas, Melinda was used to playing every position from post to wing to point guard. When we recruited

RECRUITING POODLES AND PLAYERS

ONE THING COACH SHARP HAS LEARNED OVER THE YEARS IS THAT THE HAZARDS of recruiting can come from unlikely suspects. Once while on a recruiting trip to Pampa, Texas, Coach Sharp and Coach Weese were waiting patiently in the prospective player's living room while the family gathered. From down the hall, they could hear a small dog yipping, growling, and running pell-mell toward the living room. They watched, enthralled, as a poodle rounded the corner, its paws furiously grasping for purchase on the slick linoleum. Making a beeline for Coach Sharp, the dog didn't wait for an exchange of greetings, but bared its teeth and clamped down solidly on the top of her instep. Coach Sharp, trying not to alert the family to her peril, shook her foot up and down, all the while clenching her teeth to keep from yelling, but the poodle would not let go. Coach Weese jumped up to help get the dog off before any of the family appeared or his boss passed out from pain. Eventually the two dislodged the dog. In the end, though, the player was not signed and Coach Sharp left the visit with not only a sore foot, but holes in her hose.

her, we saw her potential as a point guard and wanted to hone her great gift of leadership both on and off the court. Melinda possessed this gift innately, but didn't use it to its full extent until she became a Lady Raider. Her leadership and inspiration on the court were a constant throughout her tenure with us, whether we were tied or behind by thirty points. She and I even began to share a pre-game ritual. For some reason, I have always had the unfortunate habit of being extremely nauseous before games, even after twenty-plus years of coaching. Melinda always had the habit of having extremely sweaty hands right before we went on the court. When I would shake her hands during player introductions, I'd say, "Okay, we're ready to play—your hands are sweaty." She would fire back at me, "Have you thrown up yet?" If I said yes, she knew I was ready to play, too. There was one instance when we were playing in conference tournament in Kansas City where she was the one who was nauseous. She seemed quite ill to me, so I asked her if we needed to start someone else. Melinda said absolutely not, that she would be okay. She went out and played an intense thirty-five minutes for us that day. Determination combined with a play-to-win mentality made her invaluable as a player, and that same go-to combination continues in her, even now as one of our assistant coaches. Discovering her leadership on and off the court has been a thrill for all of us.

Helping players perfect their talents is one of the delights of coaching.

However, if the coach senses a glaring flaw during the recruiting process, it is better to walk away, rather than to expect a drastic change in a player. The old saying that "you don't change the stripes on a tiger" is quite realistic when dealing with basic character issues. Every coach would admit to mistakes in judging an athlete, which later led to an uncomfortable relationship. At the same time, any coach could give examples of how a player worked out better than expected. I could give several examples of times when I felt shaky at best about signing a certain player. Each time I went against my instincts, I really paid a price.

One such example occurred several years ago. During an in-home visit, I asked a recruit a question about whether she had ever watched a couple of other players who were going to be a part of our program. She replied that she really wasn't interested in the other players; she was only concerned about her own playing. Obviously, a red flag went up, but I didn't follow my feelings. We signed her. Sure enough, it was evident daily that she had meant what she said. Her entire focus was on her own situation, and it was rather difficult for her to become team-oriented. She had some solid attributes, which included an incredible work ethic and discipline, but she had very little interest in building our team. I blame myself as much as anyone because I went against my gut feeling about her "fit." Lesson learned!

Above all, the most important aspect in recruiting a team in any field is to take as few risks as possible in order to insure the program's integrity. It takes much time, energy, and thought to find the players who fit into your program's philosophy and share your vision. I believe that life is too short to spend it in conflict with underachievers. I have been fortunate enough in my career to coach individuals who have exemplified true POWER; they have made the success of the Lady Raider program possible and the coaching profession a joy.

RECRUITING PEOPLE AND PLAYERS

Stephanie Scott Gerber

GUARD

1990-1994

Plano, Texas

WHEN STEPHANIE SCOTT GERBER ANTICIpated being courted by recruiters, she always assumed she would choose to become an Aggie like her parents. Because she had never been exposed to the Texas Panhandle much at all and had only heard about its rather sparse landscape, she thought, "Why would I want to go out to the desert to play basketball?" On the other hand, she wanted to play for a program known for its winning tradition, and she wanted to play in the Southwest Conference. At that time, Coach Sharp's teams had never finished lower than third in the Southwest Conference. After visiting both Tech and Texas A&M numerous times, however, Stephanie noticed that Texas Tech always recruited positively—no derision of other school's programs, coaches, or players. She also sensed that their players always seemed to enjoy each other. For instance, on one recruiting trip, Coach Weese recognized that Scott had a penchant for humor. Instead of resorting to belittling other players and teams in an effort to win her over, he arranged for Stephanie

and another recruit named Kim Pruitt to go see a funny movie and get to know each other better. On a last trip to A&M before her signing decision had to be made, the pressure from both schools was very great. While driving around the A&M campus, Stephanie quietly prayed to herself, "Please, God, just show me a sign, just a little sign that will let me know what you want me to do and where you want me to go." At that moment, Stephanie says she looked up to one of the street signs on campus. It said Lubbock! That was the beginning of Stephanie's life at Texas Tech. She was a member of the 1993 National Championship Team, but quips with her trademark sense of humor, "I led the airball record." Stephanie continues to live in Lubbock and can be seen at most home games sitting behind the north goal of the United Spirit Arena, corralling her two young boys, Garrett and Grayson. Every now and then, she'll steal a look at the 1993 Championship banner and voice another prayer. This time, it's one not of desperation, but of gratitude.

Scrappy Stephanie Scott's typical uniform always included knee-pads.

3

CHEMISTRY

1988–1989
Lady Raider Average Home Game Attendance: 1,485

Basketball is jazz: improvisatory, free, individualistic,
corporate, sweaty, fast, exulting screeching, torrid,
explosive, exquisitely designed for letting first the trumpet,
then the sax, then the drummer, then the
trombonist soar away in virtuoso excellence.

MICHAEL NOVAK, *The Joy of Sports*

REATING POSITIVE CHEMISTRY IS, PERHAPS, THE most important leadership skill a person can have. Chemistry separates good teams from great teams, and if not established firmly, can diminish a great team into an underachieving team in a hurry. In other words, it can define a team quicker than any other element. If I were able to tell you exactly how to accomplish good chemistry, I would probably be in another business, but I absolutely know what it looks like and how to recognize when it isn't there.

Diversity within the ranks of any organization forces a leader to work hard to find common ground. From a coaching standpoint it is common to have team members from many different locales. Some players come from small close-knit communities, while others hail from complex urban environments. As you can imagine, these pre-college worlds are drastically different. It takes time for teammates to develop common ground, and they need help from both team leaders and coaches to accomplish this task.

Everything great within any team setting begins with relationships. The best type of team relationship has much more to do with respect than it does with affection. Great friends do not necessarily make great teams, even though playing with friends is fun and much easier. However, strong teammates must, without fail, respect each other's talents and commitment to the greater good of the group. Respecting someone whom you do not like very much is difficult, especially when you are a young adult and have not learned much tolerance for unfamiliar people or situations. Learning to accept others, learning to understand diversity, and learning to assimilate new situations are invaluable lessons taught better in sports than in any other arena of our society. It is part of a coach's mission to guide players through this learning process where, hopefully, respect begins to make its appearance, a team will be strengthened, and the seeds of positive chemistry start to grow.

The path from mutual respect to good chemistry is a journey based on several factors that vary from year to year and even from day to day. For instance, with a veteran team, much of the groundwork is already in place because the players share a history. The biggest question here is what kind

Lady Raiders relax in Monaco.

of history? If the history is negative, the path to positive chemistry is more difficult than if the team has no history together at all. My experience is that even veterans must spend some time together, one-on-one, to learn to appreciate each other, to be honest with each other, and to work out existing negative factors. Often the coach has to be involved at least on the perimeter to help mediate these discussions. Sometimes, the roots of these problems involve a whole network of people, and there must be an objective mediator, who has the group's best interest at heart, to direct this process. Even if the pre-existing chemistry is strong, there is no guarantee that it will stay that way if it isn't constantly nurtured. Just because a child is a good kid doesn't mean that she will always remain so, no matter how much, or how little, guidance and attention she gets. It is a constant process for that child to continue to flourish. It is the same for any relationship in life—teammates are no exception.

Building relationships among players on a new team creates an entirely different set of circumstances. This takes some very specific planning and creative approaches and should be a priority for everyone. The leadership must never downplay its importance. From the beginning, players have to know what the goal is and that there is no hidden agenda. One of the most useful tools in accomplishing this task is simply spending time together— learning about each other, learning what makes their teammates tick, discovering what they like and dislike, etc. This information could include anything as non-threatening as finding out what kind of ice cream they like to something

Tech cheerleaders ignite the crowd with "Raider Power."

as important as what their biggest dreams are. We need to learn about families, faiths, backgrounds, fears, expectations, goals, personality traits that we like and those we don't—especially those we don't. Only then can we begin to deal with obstacles that have the potential to become roadblocks.

One way we tackle this objective in Lady Raider basketball is to set up specific team-building events. These are informal, casual gatherings where players feel comfortable. We get together to play games or to cookout, or maybe just to sit around and talk. Whatever the event, the goal is to bond off the court. One year, some of the juniors and seniors got together on their own and chose one night per week when one player would cook dinner for the others, rotating cooks throughout the season. Not only does this time commitment build team chemistry, it also creates common ground (as well as memorable and, I'm told, not-so-memorable meals together.)

Another important part of the chemistry process is to share thoughts that you as a leader believe to be important. Together, watch a movie that conveys a message your team needs to hear, or have every player read a book that addresses a certain skill you want your team to learn. We've also engaged speakers to talk to the group about unity, tradition, or anything else appropriate. The point is to have some group activities that encourage them to talk collectively about the values important to the team's development.

While putting teammates together in comfortable settings builds mutual trust, putting them together in uncomfortable situations can be just as effective. For instance, the Lady Raiders get many invitations to speak for various community events. We will purposely accept one at a school and send a couple of our young players together to speak. For many of them, it is their first time to do anything quite that scary. Players bond quickly in the reality of challenges like that. They rely on each other for confidence and moral support if nothing else. They usually come back with funny stories about what one or the other did on that first speaking engagement.

Making efficient use of practice time and providing varied court opportunities for players to bond is another way to develop and strengthen chemistry. We do everything from creating competitions within the team to monitoring strenuous activities that make players rely on each other. It is crucial, when directing competitive activities, to team up different players constantly. For instance, if we play a shooting game, there are many ways to divide the squad. One day we might divide up into classes—upper classmen v. lower classmen. The next day we might put our senior leaders together with our freshmen or our guards against our post players in order to encourage bonding with different people every day. Rewarding the winners of a competition should be meaningful, but also fun. Maybe the reward is a workout t-shirt or not having to run a set of conditioning drills. Perhaps the losers have to serve the winners at the next team meal. All of these incentives add an element of anticipation and a belief that winning produces rewards—a positive mentality that is crucial for the entire season.

Obviously, game time is the most important opportunity to encourage chemistry. Players must learn to rely on each other throughout the entire forty minutes of competition. Sometimes, in early season games, a coach needs to let the team figure out their own chemistry. They have to learn that when they are on the court, they are responsible for each other. For instance, if you have a defensive possession in which one player gets beaten and needs help to stop the opponent, make your team learn to depend on each other— to "get each other's back" as the saying goes.

The same is true on the offensive end of the floor as well. It is crucial for a team to know who the "go-to" players are. Some players have talent, but no tenacity. Others have more guts than ability. Go-to players have both—that rare confidence-inspiring combination that pushes them to take the big, game-deciding shot. These "money-players," as I like to call them, have ice water in their veins and can be depended on in the tough times. Once the coaches have pinpointed these players, it is imperative to make all the team members aware of them and direct the team not to accept any other player's inclinations to put herself in that place.

One year at Texas Tech our failure to execute this important go-to player objective cost us a very important game. We were playing in a conference tournament championship game against the University of Texas in Dallas' Reunion Arena. The game was tied; we had the basketball with thirty seconds left in the game. I called a timeout and called for a specific play. We wanted to hold the ball until the last five seconds before attempting a shot. The worst scenario would be overtime and the best would be that we would win at the buzzer. Our coaching staff asked for any questions, trying to make sure that everyone was on the same page. We thought we were ready. After the timeout, we in-bounded the ball to our point guard who let some seconds run off the clock, just as we had planned. However, instead of running the play that was designed to allow one of our go-to post players to attempt the last shot with about ten seconds left, the guard attempted a shot at the three-point line. She missed; the Longhorns rebounded, advanced down the floor, and shot at the buzzer to win. Our entire team was stunned. This game remains one of my most disappointing losses for two reasons. One, we should have won, or at least gone into overtime. Second, I failed to demand the discipline necessary to execute that critical possession. Some lessons are tough to learn.

On the flip side, a couple of years later in the same arena and in the same tournament, we were playing an excellent University of Houston team in a semi-final game on the way to the championship. This time we were down by one point with about twenty seconds left in the game. Again, we called a time-out and set a play, an isolation screen and roll. We decided to execute it with freshman guard Rene Hanebutt and post player Michi Atkins. This time our players reacted perfectly and Hanebutt scored to give us the win with about two seconds left. This team had learned the importance of the go-to player and had found the discipline necessary to make the big play.

One of the most important ingredients in creating strong chemistry within any team is to make sure the players understand their roles. A coach is a great help to her players if she is able to define and communicate to each individual her particular role on the team. This can obviously be a very delicate issue because everyone thinks she would like to be the star. In reality, very few players actually are equipped to be the go-to player. However, it is important at the college level, where every player has been used to star status at home, to communicate role information in a way that does not destroy a player's ability to contribute. Even though she may not be the prime focus of a team, every player can contribute in a significant way. This role definition is an ongoing challenge, which must be met by any successful coaching staff.

For this role information to be communicated effectively, preparation is essential. First of all, a staff must decide which role best fits each player. This may sound easy, but you want to be certain that you have read all of your options well. For instance, you do not want to spend an entire pre-season believing a person will be your go-to player only to find out that in the thick of action, that individual does not have the necessary mental steel. Careful consideration and past experiences must all be taken into account before this decision is made, because it will make the difference in winning close games or losing. Not only will the 'chosen' one have to be comfortable with this coveted role, but somehow that individual, along with the coaching staff, will have to earn the trust of all of their teammates.

Equally important is communicating your expectations to every single member of the team. If it is clear, for instance, that a player will not be a starter, a coach must make that player feel as valuable as the go-to player. Failure to do this will destroy the infrastructure of the squad. Team sports as well as other organizations must be all-inclusive. Everyone must feel needed and must feel some ownership, not only of this particular team, but of the program as a whole. Individual sessions involving the coach and each player will be the most crucial part of this process. The coach should be very clear about what that player's focus should be, not only in practice, but also in the games. For instance, if you have a very athletic guard who is your best defensive player, but does not shoot the ball very well, it is important that she feel ownership of defending the best perimeter player on the other team. She must also understand, however, that she is maybe the fifth option on the offensive end. It is imperative here that a coach handle this revelation with tact so that the great defensive attributes become the focus rather than the lack of offensive skills. Not only does this player need to feel that her defensive skills will be a major part of any victory, but every other member of the team must recognize that truth also.

Even more difficult for a player to accept is lack of playing time. The players who fill the roles of the ninth, tenth, and lower positions on the team must also feel ownership and connection with the players who are getting the majority of the minutes, which is one of the biggest challenges a coach faces in developing good chemistry. First of all, these individuals must develop a trust in the coach, and then they must be able to put the team first in all instances, which may mean swallowing a great deal of pride. A successful coach finds ways to make these players feel important, from applauding their efforts in workout, to making them an important part of off-court activities, to confiding in them about important decisions about the team in general. When they begin to feel that kind of importance, they naturally start con-

CHEMIST, CATALYST, AND COACH

Krista Kirkland Gerlich

GUARD

1989–1993
Spearman, Texas

ABOUT HALFWAY DOWN MIMOSA STREET IN Hereford, Texas, was the home of a champion. Some of the neighbors might not have known this, however. They probably knew, because of the cutout of a Hereford whiteface in the front yard, that the woman who lived there was the wife of the Hereford Whitefaces' football coach, Bryan Gerlich, and one of "The Herd's" most faithful cheerleaders. They knew her as the thirty-something mother of two beautiful children, Bryn and Brayden, who played in the front yard. Or they knew her as the high school math teacher who made pre-calculus rather  challenging for some of Hereford's best students. Not many of the neighbors knew, however, that living within shouting distance of them was the heart and soul of the 1993 Lady Raider National Championship team—Krista Kirkland

Gerlich—whose trademark "backdoor" assist passes to Sheryl Swoopes became their habitual joy during the 1993 season.

There was a time when there was no need to reveal that she was a former champion Lady Raider. Everyone knew it. How could anyone who breathed West Texas air not know it within three to four years of 1993? Now, more than a decade later, the "hoopla" has faded a bit, but the news was still wondrously fun to let slip, and she saw her students' eyes widen and expressions freeze as they pondered the import of such news from their lovely and graceful pre-cal teacher.

Krista is a native West Texan, having grown up in the West Texas towns of Sudan and Spearman. A basketball coach's daughter, she honed her skills in both towns' high school gyms, especially on summer days when the gyms were relatively empty. She would go there to shoot for three or four hours, and then the "lunch bunch" would show up, mostly black guys on break who went to the gym for a quick pick-up game before going back to work. Oftentimes they would ask Krista to join them for a game or two. Then break would be over, and she would spend three or four more hours shooting the ball, getting the rhythm right, practicing. Just practicing—not noticing the time at all. Those idyllic high school days would race back to her mind a few years later when Coach Sharp called her over during a Lady Raider workout and asked impatiently, "Why is it that in high school y'all spent so much time in the gym practicing and in college y'all show up ten minutes before practice, put your shoes on, work out, and then ten minutes after practice you're out the door? Why is that?" Krista knew then that it was time to get back to the fundamentals, that perhaps practice really would make perfect, and that one of the fundamental elements necessary to achieve as a Lady Raider under Coach Marsha Sharp was work ethic. It is the single most important lesson she gleaned from her years at Texas Tech.

Krista's decision to sign with Texas Tech was a studied one. Two important exchanges helped her reach her decision. One occurred with her father's assistant coach, Carla Flowers. Carla had played under Coach Sharp at Lockney High School and her only comment when Krista asked what she thought of Coach Sharp was, "If she told me to run through a brick wall, I would do it." The other exchange was a number. Krista grew up watching Lisa Wood in Sudan, who later played for Texas Tech and wore #21. Wood's commitment to basketball was indelibly evident to Krista; Woods knew the necessity of going above and beyond what is required, the "extras" of achieving greatness. In honor of her hometown basketball idol, Krista asked to wear #21 for the Lady Raiders. The fact that the retired #21 jersey hangs in the United Spirit Arena today not only honors Krista Kirkland Gerlich, but also attests to the influence of Lisa Wood.

Krista remembers that the factor most impressive to her during her recruitment was the Lady Raider coaches' honesty and candor. There were no "fluff and puff" recruiting tactics. It was simple, straightforward, and fair. She recalls that the highly politicized tactics used by other schools' recruiters included suggesting that Krista would be one of the top five recruits and would surely be able to play. Coach Sharp's method was to say that she wanted Krista as a shooting guard behind Karen Farst and that, if she wanted a spot badly enough, she could fight for it, and it would be hers. There was no hierarchy of commitment due to class rank. Work ethic, along with integrity, was central when Krista signed the papers to go to Texas Tech in the fall of 1989.

Her freshman year at Texas Tech was not a year that Krista would remember fondly. It was quite an adjustment, and there were some distracting team dynamics running in the background of workouts. Some players were just not sure if they were going to stick around to complete their scholarships, and some parents were disappointed in the amount of playing time "their girls" were receiving. Coach Sharp acknowledged little of this frustration, until one morning in the spring of the season when Krista got a call at 8:30 AM from her coach. She answered the phone and heard Coach Sharp's voice. "So, Krista, are you going to play with us or not? I have a vision for the Lady Raider program, and I need to know if you are with us." Krista gulped and said, "Well, yes, uh, Coach Sharp. I'm with you. Whatever you need me to do. I'm here to stay." Later, Krista, then a sophomore, was stunned to hear that she had the green light as far as shot selection was concerned. "Whenever you feel like you have a good look and a chance to score, take it," said Coach Sharp. That moment of trust was essential in her development as a leader on the court. Coach Reding told her during practice that she had to keep shooting: "Even though you miss the first six, you have to believe that the next six are going to go in." That summer of her sophomore year, Krista went back to the gym in Spearman, spending the shooting hours necessary for a champion to evolve.

Four other players of the team got the same "house cleaning" phone call that spring. Teresa McMillan, Jennifer

Buck, Tami Walker, and Alexis Ware all went home that summer committed to honing the fundamental skills that got them their scholarships in the first place. When this Texas Tech team beat the heretofore unbeatable University of Texas the next season in the Southwest Conference semifinals, Krista knew that something special was going to happen while she was at Tech. And, at that point, this 1990–1991 Lady Raider team didn't even know Sheryl Swoopes. They had created this chemistry by themselves. Krista remembers, "We went on to get slaughtered by Arkansas in the finals, but we had beaten Texas. To me, that was the birth of the 1993 National Championship team."

Years later, in the summer of 2003, Coach Sharp made another phone call to Krista. The Lady Raiders were again in need of her unique gifts in terms of leadership, inspiration, and accountability. They needed an assistant coach. Krista had had a previous conversation with Coach Sharp about this possibility, but had begun to think it wasn't going to happen. The day Sharp called, Krista was involved in a rather damaging car wreck and was completely distraught. When husband Bryan came to pick her up, he told her that Sharp had called and that Krista was to call her on her cell phone. She made the call to Sharp, and after some pleasantries, Sharp said, "Okay, you, can you hear me? I'm standing by some fountains, but I want you to be sure you can hear every word I say. I've been waiting for ten years to ask you this question: Would you come be my assistant coach for the Lady Raiders?" Krista completely forgot about the wreck in that moment. She remembers, "I went from the lowest low to the highest high in all of about 30 seconds, and I think all I did was scream." When Krista calmed down enough to say "Yes!" she could hear Coach Sharp's entire entourage singing the Texas Tech fight song in the background. "My biggest dream came true that day," Krista recalls.

The day the 2003–2004 team began its initial practices, Lady Raider assistant coach, Krista Kirkland Gerlich, taped a memo to the front of each player's locker. It read, "What are you doing right now to make your dream of a national championship come true?" Perhaps with one of the Lady Raiders' best chemists back in the lab, the team can again make history.

Krista Kirkland in action against Baylor.

tributing to the chemistry of the team.

Hopefully, the older players on a team are getting minutes and younger players are attempting to learn the ropes behind the older players whom they respect and admire. If that is the case, the coach's job becomes somewhat easier. The staff should direct much time and energy toward keeping young players connected and focused on the future, working with them daily and individually to ensure that improvement occurs. This, too, results in a powerful, positive chemistry which will continue throughout the season.

Obviously, role definition is a different process and challenge with every season. However, as I said earlier, chemistry is about relationships. Defining roles will not be effective unless a coach and her staff have taken the time not only to evaluate the skills of their team, but also to take stock of each individual's personality, commitment, and mentality. Time spent on this important front end will have immeasurable value throughout the challenges of the season.

Once team roles are defined, it will be much easier to make sure the whole team is focused on achieving common goals. As this is one of the most important aspects of a program, the coaching staff must be very involved in the entire process. It is a delicate situation. You can't allow a goal to be so lofty that it is unrealistic and would cause a team to lose its identity. On the other hand, teams usually will only progress as high as their goals are placed. Setting goals too low, then, might produce a team of underachievers. While it is definitely a difficult chore to find the perfect balance for a team, it can be done and its importance cannot be overstated.

The short-term goals must be set from the very beginning. Let's say that a long-term goal for a team may be to win a conference title. That's great, but if it's October and practices are just beginning, the reality of that goal is a long way off. Therefore, it's vital to provide something in the immediate future that gains the group's focus. Maybe a staff will want to keep shooting statistics during a workout in order to intensify the effort. Maybe an early intrasquad scrimmage should have specific goals attached, so that the team's attention is directed toward the day's immediate successes.

The process employed in the Lady Raider program involves a variety of steps. First of all, as we get close to the season, we try to divide the schedule into four parts. We set goals for the pre-conference schedule, for our regular season conference race, for our conference tournament, and then for the NCAA tournament. I've found that these divisions are helpful for a staff in terms of management and achievement. It also provides a built-in clean slate several times throughout the season. For instance, if your non-conference season didn't go as well as you had hoped, you can begin again with regular conference play. On the other hand, if you played really well in non-conference games, it gives a staff the chance to shift focus from that success to the more difficult tasks still ahead. This strategy also helps players deal with being overconfident if they have to begin building again at each division.

Goals should also be broken down within each game itself. We ask ourselves the following questions: How many points will be acceptable for the other team to score? What percentage do we want our team to shoot? How many turnovers can we stand? This goal-setting brings the focus down to the immediate task at hand and can get your team inherently programmed to create a goals-driven mentality. The rewards of these small victories go a long way toward building the winning chemistry for which every team strives.

It actually may be that the most effective long-term goals are not established until it is clear how some of the short-term goals are being handled. Until a team actually goes to war, there are many variables that make it difficult to ascertain what will happen within a season. That said, in addition to practice goals and season goals, there must always be program goals. These are the targets that never change and are non-negotiable. At Texas Tech, I want every player who chooses to be a Lady Raider to come to practice each day with the mentality that we are chasing a national championship. Period. They should always feel that goal is possible. Why should teams practice on a daily basis for the reward of mediocrity? Obviously, this mindset is not always accomplished, but the mentality must be there not only from our players, but our staff, our support staff, our administration, and our fans. This goal is paramount and cannot be dismissed as too far-reaching or unrealistic. Other non-negotiable season goals at Texas Tech are:

- winning at least twenty games in a season
- winning our conference and the conference tournament
- appearing in a regional tournament in the NCAA tournament

That's it. No room for discussion. When we initially recruit players with these statements, they arrive knowing what the expectations are. Focusing players on common, non-negotiable goals is a major step in building not only great chemistry, but also great programs. We expect individuals in our program to understand these goals and to deliver them. I talk to our team repeatedly about being accountable. Successful businesses all over our country build their business concepts around accountability. If we are not accountable, we lose the urgency and daily focus necessary to become champions. From the first day a player is a part of the team, the expectations should be clear. At Texas Tech, it is made undeniably clear that, academically, there are no excuses for absences from classes, study halls, practices, team meetings, or treatments for injuries. Teaching accountability and its by-product, time management, is one of the most difficult challenges of coaching. I do believe that the consequences for failure to comply with accountability standards should be severe enough to eliminate repeat offenders.

Accountability, however, goes much deeper than deadlines. Its highest form is a player's loyalty to her team and her willingness to do whatever it takes to make that team successful. If it means spending long hours of extra work to improve a shot, or to handle the basketball better, so be it. If it means a player's taking responsibility for herself when dealing with a teammate, then get it done. Regrettably, this high form of accountability is becoming more and more difficult to find in our current society. Blaming our mistakes on someone else is not only non-productive for society at large, but it is devastating for a team. Encouraging personal responsibility is one of the greatest life lessons a coach has the opportunity to teach.

Accountability, then, is a happy by-product of positive chemistry as teammates begin to understand the effects of their choices on the entire team. Creating accountability is done not only through the coach and the staff, but through team leadership. There is no question that sometimes peers can convince other peers about accountability more effectively than anyone else. It's one thing if the coach is mad at you, but it is another thing entirely if your buddy is upset. There is no question that the greatest teams I have had the opportunity to coach also contained the greatest leaders. There is no substitute for this kind of internal leadership. Sometimes this leadership chemistry comes from one strong individual and sometimes it can be "by committee," but when it occurs, life gets better in a hurry. When a coach recognizes this leadership gift in a player, it is very important that the coach give the player enough leeway to make decisions and lead. Letting a young leader know that you trust her and that you will back her gives her the freedom and confidence to step into that role. That discovery is an incredible experience for both coaches and players.

It is no coincidence, then, that the best team chemistry I have ever witnessed at Texas Tech also happened to include the best team leader I have ever known. This was the 1993 National Championship Team. The leader's name was Krista Kirkland, and I probably learned more by watching her work that year than she learned from me. First of all, she is a coach's kid, and I usually love to coach those players because they have a special understanding

A reunion of champs — Krista Kirkland Gerlich, Sheryl Swoopes, and Marsha Sharp.

of both sides of the whistle. From a coach's perspective, I have never had another player who literally focused on me during a game's timeouts more than Krista did. She also tried to help me with team situations off the floor when she thought she could make a difference. She did something else which boosted my confidence every day: She completely sold out to our coaches and our system. If we had told her to run through a brick wall, she would have turned and started running. There was no second-guessing here, no look of disagreement, not anything but total respect. Never during her four years did that respect change.

Not only was Krista invaluable from a coach's perspective, everyone associated with our team embraced her. Our fans loved her, her professors loved her, and maybe most importantly, her teammates loved her. As I watched her that year, there were many things she did to develop team chemistry, confidence, and trust within our unit. She showed interest in every single member of the team. If a player had a history test, she remembered and would ask how it went. If a teammate went home for the weekend, she would ask about her family. If a player didn't feel well, Krista tried to help her find the medication she needed. It didn't matter what the situation was—in everything she was building relationships and, therefore, strong chemistry.

In 1991, we had an exceptional player arrive on our team who eventually became the National Player of the Year in 1993, Sheryl Swoopes. Many people have told me that Sheryl could have led any team to a national title. I have always answered that I wasn't sure that was true. She is certainly talented enough to win that title, but it was the team concept that made it possible for her to do it at Texas Tech. It took a special group to allow her the freedom to perform all the feats she did for us. Any selfishness at all could have undermined the whole process. We had a great group of players before she arrived, better players than most realized at the time, but I will always believe that the leadership Krista provided them was the link that bonded us all together.

It was amazing how much respect Sheryl and Krista had for each other. It was as if Sheryl provided the momentum by making huge plays and giving her teammates the credit, and Krista glued everyone together and took care of Sheryl in the process. Krista was Sheryl's biggest fan and made sure all of their teammates respected this unique opportunity, which in turn, led to the freedom Sheryl felt to make plays. She knew that, more than anything, everyone around her recognized her gift and wanted to help her develop it.

With this instilled confidence, Sheryl delivered what I believe to be one of the greatest individual efforts ever made in the history of women's basketball. She deserved all of the attention and accolades she received for that wonderful effort. Always in my heart, however, not only will I admire Sheryl's unbelievable ability to excel in any game, but also the equally unbelievable leadership skills of Krista Kirkland. She was an honorable mention All-American in her own right, but most importantly in my book, they were national champions together. Their retired jerseys hang together in Lubbock's United Spirit Arena today—an apt name for an arena which was realized in part because of their initial chemistry, commitment, talent, and achievement. No Texas Tech women's basketball player will ever again wear either number 21 or 22. They not only changed my life, but also the Lady Raider program for all the years to come. I am daily grateful for the opportunity to have coached such incredible players.

Assistant coaches Roger Reding and Krista Gerlich discuss
strategy for the 2003-2004 Lady Raider team.

SUCCESS

1991–1992
Lady Raider Average Home Game Attendance: 4,201

Athletic proficiency is a mighty good servant,
and like so many other good servants, a mighty bad master.
THEODORE ROOSEVELT

"The reward for work well done is the opportunity to do more."

Jonas Salk

HE 1993 NATIONAL CHAMPIONSHIP LADY Raider team was a perfect example of chemistry—when elements were melded together, when roles were understood, when internal leadership prevailed, when goals were accomplished, when all things within and without our team came together. Looking back at the mysterious and glorious ways that season unfolded still makes me shake my head in disbelief. However, the lessons we learned that season changed our program forever.

Ironically, the first game we played in the 1992–1993 season was a game at Stanford, where they dropped the National Championship banner they had won the preceding season. It was a wonderful celebration, and I wondered how it would feel to accomplish that kind of feat. Little did I imagine, though, that we would be doing the very same thing the next season. We lost the Stanford game, 65–72, but we did some significant things against a special team. I am never pleased when we lose, but I was encouraged by the way we competed and thought Sheryl Swoopes really stepped up and made some plays that gave us a chance to win. She had taken her game to some highly regarded athletes on a national stage; I knew we would need that kind of focused mentality throughout our season. The only other loss we had in non-conference play was to Utah. We were in Salt Lake City in the middle of a blizzard. We just never got on track, and Utah played very well, beating us soundly, 72–55. It was a great wake-up call for us and probably refocused us for Southwest Conference play.

We went through conference play with the usual ups and downs. I have always felt that conference play in any year is more about being a test of endurance than it is about winning every game. The last loss we suffered that year was to the University of Texas at home. It was a physical game, which is usually the case when we get together. I told Coach Jody Conradt after that season that her Lady Longhorns might have been the best team we played before facing Ohio State in the national championship game. The loss to Texas came down to a block-charge call against Krista Kirkland in the last few seconds; they capitalized on that by hitting some crunch-time

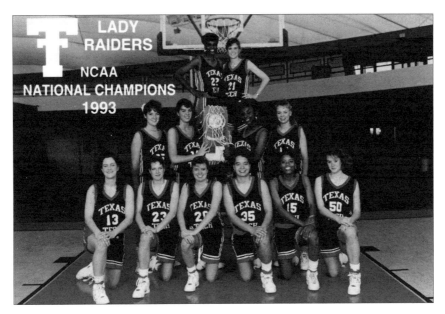

The 1993 National Championship Team.

free-throws. We ended up losing the game by one point, 75–76, but were determined not to let it happen again in that season.

The other two games we played against Texas that season really set the tone for the run through the NCAA tournament. The first one was our second regular season game against them—this time in Austin. In the history of our program, we had never beaten them on their home court. That season, Krista Kirkland took it as a personal challenge to do just that before she left Texas Tech. It was apparent in the days leading up to the trip that she was passionate about accomplishing that goal. I have said that she was the best leader that I have ever coached and, at this point her senior year, she really began to provide a model and a mentality that took us to an entirely different level. The confidence she and Sheryl had in each other became more obvious everyday.

Playing in Austin is always a challenge, however. Regardless of the sport or the venue, it's always a real Texas showdown. They have terrific fans, too, who take their team personally. We always have to remind our team to take the crowd out of the game, and disregard the many unfavorable comments thrown at us. The same is true for them when they visit Lubbock; there is no question both teams bring a little extra enthusiasm to our annual match-ups. The moment we took the floor, it was evident how much electricity was in the air, especially since the Longhorn loyal remembered that Swoopes had traded in her burnt-orange jersey for red and black. Winning in Austin is still one of the most special times I have ever experienced. It was almost as if they were not going to be denied and whatever they needed to do, or whenever they needed to provide a lift to their teammates, it happened. Our fans went crazy and were a huge part of our victory. The game at Texas was a war, but in the end, we made enough plays and beat them by ten points, 76–66. One of my favorite snapshot moments of the '93 experience was when we left the arena in Austin that night. Krista and Sheryl were walking down the walkway with their arms around each other's shoulders and huge smiles on their faces. They realized that we just might be something special.

The other game we played against the Longhorns that year was in the finals of the Conference Tournament. The scene was Reunion Arena in Dallas. The crowd was split right down the middle with burnt-orange on one half and red and black on the other, as if the eyes of all of Texas were on that game. Even the university bands began to have it out, filling the air with "Fight Raiders Fight" and "The Eyes of Texas." Two Tech trombone players even wore cutout basketballs on their heads while they played! Both teams were gearing up for post-season play and sparring for bragging rights. Unusual for our rivalry, they had beaten us in Lubbock by one point, and we had won in Austin—this gave both teams extra incentive to win. I can honestly say that game provided as good an atmosphere as there is in the nation for women's basketball. Texas jumped out to a seventeen-point lead early; we really had to dig deep to have a chance to win. I have never witnessed a more passionate performance from any athlete in any sport than what Sheryl Swoopes did that day. She finished with 53 points and really began a three-week journey that may never be matched by a women's basketball player. She rebounded, played defense, shot free throws, and was definitely in a zone. She wove through the Longhorn defense with her signature speed and grace, finding the open teammate for a pass or driving through the paint and putting the ball up herself. For the fans watching her play, it was truly a thing of beauty to see the game played as it was meant to be—she was finesse personified. She literally took over the game and encouraged her teammates to play beyond themselves as well. The entire team played as one, nailing quick fingertip passes, shutting down the Longhorn offense, finding the open man, and running from end to end with dizzying speed. It was a nationally televised contest, and for the first time, people across the country thought that Texas Tech might be a team to watch. We beat the Longhorns in Dallas that day, 78–71, and won the tournament. Our fans were ecstatic. All of a sudden, the questions from the media changed. Instead of asking, "Now, exactly *where is* Lubbock?" reporters began to ask, "Do you think this team can play with the *best* teams in the country?" "Do you think you *really* have a *chance* to get to Atlanta?" "How *far* do you think Swoopes can take this team?" The atmosphere sparked with electricity. Returning to Lubbock, we could feel the hope begin to rise, and local folks began to joke about the sweet smell of Georgia peaches. Little did I dream what the next few weeks would hold.

The next day was Selection Sunday for the NCAA Tournament, which we watched with great interest and anticipation. Our first game was to be played in Lubbock against the Washington Huskies. If we won that contest, we would be in a bracket with USC, University of Colorado, and the number one seed in the west, Stanford. We immediately gathered films and sent coaches on the road to watch opponents, which was at that time legal in NCAA play. We rested our team for a few days and then got ready to play Washington, coached by Chris Gobrecht. The team was known for a very tough and aggressive man-to-man defense and quick-hit offense. We had maybe the closest and toughest game of the tournament against them. Sheryl stunned her knee early in the first half after running a fastbreak, chasing a slightly overthrown pass. As the ball was going out of bounds under the basket, she over-extended and crashed into the pad. She clung to the goal for a few seconds, her faced twisted in pain. I will always remember the nauseous feeling in the pit of my stomach, and the eerie silence in the Lubbock Coliseum. All of us hoped this was not a season-ending injury. I think the team knew how serious a blow this might be, but they were also a group of overachievers who weren't easily taken down. During the subsequent time-outs, they would look down the bench toward Sheryl and try to assess where we were. Then they looked straight into my eyes, focusing on the information we were giving them and did exactly as they had done all season—they made the plays necessary for victory. We played several minutes without Sheryl, but our team regrouped with remarkable poise. We held off a couple of tough Washington runs to hold on until Sheryl felt good enough to get back in the game. Freshman center Michi Atkins had a great game for us that day and was not to be denied under the basket. The Huskies began to have several scoreless possessions, discouraged in large part by our crazed Lady Raider crowd. It was a battle from start to finish, but we were fortunate enough to be the victors by six points, 70-64. When we finally had the win, there was nothing but sheer relief on the part of everyone associated with our program. We had made it to the *Sweet Sixteen.*

Our next stop was Missoula, Montana, the site of the West Regional games of the '93 tournament. We played Southern California in the first

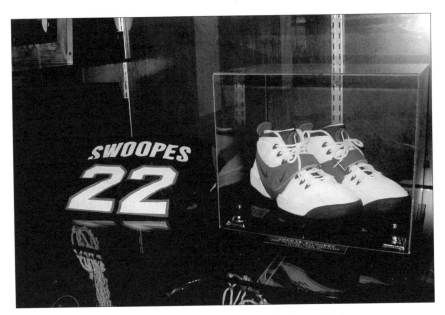

Sheryl Swoopes' jersey and signature Nike Air Swoopes™ shoes.

round, and I sat on the bench in amazement at the continued confidence level and poise our team displayed. It was almost as if they had gained a new level of maturity from the Washington game; they suddenly trusted each other and became totally unselfish, which would prove to be their most important traits the rest of the way. USC was good, and a young Lisa Leslie shared glimpses of what the future would hold for her. She made some phenomenal athletic plays and ran down the court like a gazelle. She was just beginning what all of us now recognize as a truly spectacular career. However, we were playing so solidly at this point that we were able to get a lead and never look back. Every one of our starters scored early and the 2–3 zone defense we played flowed with a sense of confidence and trust that comes only from playing an entire season together. Krista Kirkland racked up some incredible stats, making 7 out of 10 shots, 3 out of 5 three-pointers, and 9 of 11 free-throws. Her 26 points, added to Swoopes' stunning 33, gave us a sound win over the Women of Troy, 87–67. It was a great game that helped us maintain a confidence level that we would certainly need during the next ten days. It is interesting to note, too, that we were witnessing history in the making—just three years after this game, Lisa Leslie, Swoopes and several other great players that season would become the charter members of the WNBA formed in 1996. These women would play basketball on a national stage and be compensated as the professionals their talent demanded them to be.

After the win over Southern Cal, our coaches moved from the bench back to press row to scout our next opponents. Our players visited with their families and fans and then watched with great concentration and interest as Colorado played the number one seed, Stanford. Ever since the bracket announcement, I had spent several hours a day watching film on Stanford, trying to put together a game plan that I thought would give us a chance to win. I was also remembering their seven-point victory over us at the season's beginning. I felt like they were one of the best teams in the nation and that chances were good we would have to go through them to get to Atlanta. As we watched the teams play, Colorado did everything right and the former championship team, Stanford, could not catch a break. Colorado was sensational, and Shelly Sheets played one of the most inspired games I have ever witnessed. She was the guard for Colorado and made every play she had to in order to give her team a chance to win. Stanford, on the other hand, struggled all night. It was one of those times when a great team just didn't quite play up to the level they had maintained all year, and Colorado played its best game of the season. I remember the minutes ticking off the clock, thinking about all of the hours we had spent on Stanford. I told my assistant coaches then that we were going to be playing Colorado. We were amazed at this turn of events. The Buffaloes did come through with a stunning upset of the Stanford Cardinals. Fortunately, we had covered all of our bases and had spent plenty of time studying Colorado, too. I felt like we were ready to prepare our players for the next step—*the Elite Eight.*

The next day would decide which team would have the opportunity to play in the *Final Four.* The reality of our dream was so close, we could smell it. There was incredible excitement among our entire traveling party; these faithful fans had made the long journey from Lubbock to Missoula just to watch us play, doing their part to help us win.

Missoula is a beautiful, small city, and the weather was great. Not far from where we were staying was a hill. (In West Texas, we would call it a small mountain.) Two members of our immediate traveling party were physical fitness enthusiasts: our trainer, Natalie Steadman, and our associate athletic director, Jeannine McHaney, who was already battling metastic breast cancer. Before the Southern Cal game, they decided to climb the hill and take a look at the city. Although it was a little grueling, especially for Jeannine, they thought it was worth the effort. We made a point of telling them that they had paid the price, and we would surely win, which we did. Well, we were not taking any chances for the Colorado game. They knew they had to make the trek again. The only trouble was that the weather was

OF SWOOPES, CHAMPIONS, AND THE SOUVENIRS OF SUCCESS

Sheryl Swoopes

FORWARD

1991–1993

WHEN FRESHMEN PLAYERS CAME ON BOARD with the Lady Raiders for the 2003-2004 season, they had only to look at their feet to realize they were part of something special. That season, the Lady Raiders donned a new basketball shoe, the latest Nike Air Swoopes™. Each Lady Raider was given two pairs of shoes, red for home games and black for road games. Complete with silver accents, the shoes make a sparkling statement under the bright lights of the United Spirit Arena. The Nikes were a special request of Sheryl Swoopes —1993 Lady Raider champion, two-time WNBA Most Valuable Player, and three-time Olympian. While Nike provides other collegiate teams with basketball shoes, the Lady Raiders were the only ones who could wear this particular style of Air Swoopes.

Little did anyone realize that the little girl from Brownfield, Texas, who used to hone her skills by playing against her brothers on a makeshift dirt court, would someday become an icon of women's basketball. The familiar Nike slogan, "Just Do It," seems entirely appropriate when speaking of Sheryl Swoopes; she is a fitting spokesperson for the company whose very name means "goddess of victory."

"Just Do It" is also a fitting slogan for someone who was crucial to Sheryl's success; however, the two have never met. Wanda Tyler Greenfield never thought that her drive to play basketball in Brownfield, Texas, would have such far-reaching implications. In 1944, Wanda Tyler transferred to Brownfield as a senior from O'Donnell, Texas, where she had been a basketball star, having loved and played the game since she was seven years old. However, upon enrollment in Brownfield High School, she discovered that there was no girls' basketball team. She was appalled and took it on herself to rally other interested players who took their petition to the school's principal. Their strategy worked. Wanda and her makeshift team played that year, and she went on to play for the Wayland Baptist Queens. (They hadn't even thought about being the Flying Queens yet.) Wanda just wanted to play, so she just did it, paving the way at Brownfield for the arrival of Sheryl Swoopes more than four decades later.

All of the national attention surrounding the best women's player this game has ever known still makes Lady Raider Assistant Coach Roger Reding shake his head. He remembers the incredible process by which Sheryl Swoopes found her way to the Lady Raider locker room. He was working at the time with Head Coach Lyndon Hardin at South Plains College in Levelland, Texas. They had been looking at this terrific recruit from Brownfield and had enjoyed some informal in-home visits with Swoopes' mother, Louise, and brother, Brandon. Sheryl's coming to South Plains was a long shot, they knew, but they still wanted to keep in touch. She ended up going to the University of Texas, wooed by the Longhorn's winning basketball tradition. Swoopes stayed in touch with the South Plains coaches, but little did they know that when Sheryl got to Austin, other conversations were going on as well.

Deborah Williams, a South Plains standout player, was a good friend of Swoopes and kept in close contact with her. When Sheryl called from Austin, homesick and extremely unhappy, Deborah suggested Swoopes call Coach Hardin and Coach Reding. Reding remembers, "Deborah just reminded Swoopes of the alternative of coming back to play for South Plains College, remaining close to home and then seeing what might happen after that."

It just so happened that another potential All-American at Wayland Baptist University, Carol Bailey, called South Plains during the same two-day period. So, Coach Lyndon Hardin and South Plains College signed two future All-Americans within a week. Swoopes was headed back home. "It really worked out best for everyone involved," Reding surmised. "The Lady Raiders had another chance to recruit Swoopes after she played a year at South Plains; I had been hired by the Lady Raider team by that time and so had the opportunity to remain in close contact with Swoopes until she actually made her way to Tech in the fall of 1991. You know the rest," he laughs, shaking his head.

One other memorable conversation took place during that time. Lady Raider Assistant Coach Linden Weese was playing in a golf tournament in Littlefield, Texas, when he got a call from his good friend, Lyndon Hardin. Hardin called to tell Coach Weese that South Plains had to make room in the dorm for a new transfer—Sheryl Swoopes. Weese remembers that he was about to tee off when Hardin called. When he got off the phone, Coach Weese recalls, "I stepped up to hit my tee shot and, even though it went in the water, I knocked the cover off the ball I was so excited." It was one of the longest drives he had ever hit.

As the members of the 1993 National Championship team gathered in Coach Sharp's home for a reunion brunch to celebrate the 10-year anniversary of their accomplishment, it was immediately apparent that those players had moved on in their lives, but 1993 was definitely a turning point. She had invited not only the players, but also their families to come and celebrate the 10th anniversary of the 1993 season. Some came in with basketball-players-in-the-making themselves (husbands and two or three children in tow) or away from actual basketball teams they currently coach. Cynthia Clinger Kinghorn delighted everyone with her entourage of three strapping boys, a proud husband, and the promise of another son on the way.

As they began to mingle, it was also apparent that the mysterious chemistry, which was part of that '93 team, was once again being forged among them. The bond of having done something truly special, "entirely pure" as Michelle Thomas described it, began to move among them, and they began remembering. Recalling personalities, hysterical moments, ecstatic joys, and the fun they had was part of every conversation. Sheryl Swoopes arrived a bit

A determined Sheryl Swoopes in the 1993 National Championship game.

late from Houston, but when she and 5-year-old son Jordan (named after her hero, Michael Jordan) entered, there was no fanfare for this storied WNBA star. She just came in, hugged each teammate, moved among them, worried after her son, and added her voice to a roomful of memories. Little Jordan left his mom's side and immediately began practicing his Air Jordan slam-dunks with the pint-sized goal set up in Coach Sharp's backyard.

When asked how this champions' reunion felt, Sheryl stopped for a moment, and with a bit of longing, simply said, "It feels great." She was so glad to be back among the family atmosphere she felt as a Lady Raider and admitted that the biggest difference in playing professionally for the Houston Comets was the fans. "There are professional fans, too, not the ones who used to bake cookies for the Lady Raiders," she says with a grin. Playing basketball is her job now and with that comes the underside of professional athletics, too. The constant scrutiny that accompanies celebrity is a bit hard to swallow at times, she admits. While Swoopes realizes her profession has blessed her in every way, dealing with the rise of her own star has indeed been a challenge. During her reunion reflection among fans and former teammates, Sheryl said that the celebratory day had been truly wonderful and that even after winning all kinds of championships, the great thing about the '93 win was that "it was real and the others were just not as sweet as it was here. It's always good to come home." Winning the national championship is what changed the destiny of a talented, young girl from Brownfield, Texas, and became her launching pad into women's basketball history. Swoopes summed it up as she looked over a crowd of fans, former and current players, and coaches, and humbly said, "1993

changed the course of my life. All of you made me, and I will be eternally grateful."

It was apparent to everyone in the building that reunion evening that success had been a lasting souvenir for every member of that 1993 team, albeit in varying ways. Each spoke eloquently about the place the championship had in their individual journeys following graduation from Texas Tech. Cynthia Clinger Kinghorn reflected that the most special moment before becoming a wife and mother was winning the national championship. "The best moment was coming into the packed football stadium after winning. It's sharing success that is the most important thing. We felt like royalty then, and we feel like royalty tonight." She also shared the importance of the win to her growing family. "I know for sure now that I can teach my children that they can do anything they want if they set their hearts and minds to it. A lot of people say that, but I feel I can say it with sincerity." The personalized sideline chair that Coach Sharp presented to each former player will also reinforce this winning lesson in the Kinghorn home.

Janice Farris Legan, a high school English teacher, mother, and former coach, was interested in recalling some of the more humorous moments of Lady Raider basketball. One occurred when the team was playing in San Francisco. "We got a bad call and Coach Weese did one of his characteristic leaps off the bench. Coach Sharp was squatting down beside him watching the game and he landed on her fingers. I thought we were going to have to take her to the emergency room." Another memory was of the team's walking around in Utah among snowdrifts that towered over their diminutive coach. Legan also made reference to a T-shirt the team had made, which lists Coach Sharp's top ten referee slams. She joked that since she spent a few moments on the bench, she had a unique understanding of these unique terms of endearment. In addition to the many laughable times, the importance of their incredible opportunity is not lost on Legan. Her remarks at the reunion dinner were specifically geared toward the 2002-2003 team, reminding them of their great privilege to continue the tradition of excellence found in the Lady Raider locker room.

Noel Johnson, a successful coach in her own right, spoke of this tradition in terms of its instigator, Coach Sharp. "The thing that she gave us the most was a sense of trickle-down integrity. It was the idea that we were not just players, but people who could do absolutely anything. She taught us that we were citizens in the world with great power and responsibility." To Johnson, it was amazing that this kind of greatness came in the person of one so physically small. She remembered the day upperclassman Teresa McMillan came to pick her up for practice. There dangling from McMillan's rearview mirror was a pair of Coach Sharp's tennis shoes, poised like a pair of prized baby sneakers.

Krista Kirkland Gerlich had one of the most memorable comments that evening. She stepped up to the microphone and said, "Do y'all know Sheryl Swoopes? I made her." After the laughter and applause abated, Krista recalled the actual moment of winning in Atlanta. All that she, Swoopes, and Coach Sharp could do on the court was sob together in one group hug. "It was as if our three entirely different worlds came together to accomplish something wonderful. Isn't that what life is all about?"

In November 2002, nine years after their championship run, Coach Sharp went out to her front porch and found two deliveries from UPS. Both were in rather large boxes, and she couldn't imagine what was inside. When she opened them up, in one she found a large framed #22 Houston Comets jersey signed by its wearer. In the other, she found a pair of Nike Air Swoopes basketball shoes, the style worn by the WNBA Champions. They were laced, and signed, "To Coach Sharp: Thanks for all you have done for me. Love, Sheryl."

Souvenirs of success surround Coach Sharp's home, her office, as well as her mother's collection of memorabilia. One page out of a scrapbook of Sharp's early coaching days contains a small, yellowing souvenir program from the Lockney High School Girls' Athletic Banquet. Silhouettes of two young women basketball players, one in a turn-of-the-century skirted uniform and one in a pair of 1970s style shorts, illustrate the banquet's theme: "You've come a long way, baby." The date is April 10, 1976. Pictured on the Varsity Girls page is a team of thirteen young women standing and surrounding their undersized, but enthusiastic, coach. A youthful Coach Sharp is holding a basketball, shyly smiling, and sitting cross-legged in the middle of the gym floor, a rather fierce looking, flared nostril Lockney Longhorn emblem staring up at her. Thus was the beginning of trickle-down integrity.

For Sheryl Swoopes, and all of the members of the 1993 championship season, the souvenirs of success—whether they be Air Swoopes shoes, a growing family, a struggling team, or the challenges of their various vocations—remind them of just how far they've come and spur them toward laurels yet to be enjoyed. You've come a long way, baby, indeed.

Sheryl Swoopes on her way to becoming a WNBA star.

not nearly so nice; therefore, the climb wasn't quite so pleasant, but they did what they had to do. We were convinced that our chances got better by their efforts! It was so much fun to watch everyone become engaged in what we were doing. We heard many reports of fans at home organizing game-watching parties and received tons of long distance good wishes for a win in Missoula.

As game time approached, I sensed a kind of confident calmness among our players, which I thought was a very positive attitude. The team had a great warm-up, and I felt good as we tipped off. Every Tech player was set on GO. To this day, the way they played still brings tears to my eyes. It was clear they were on a mission, a confident unit, shooting with no fear of missing. Every player we started scored before Sheryl did, as if to say for herself, "This is why I was recruited to play basketball." They passed the ball knowing each other's cuts and timing perfectly; they refused to be denied this great opportunity. That day they were the best team I have ever coached.

We had a big lead at halftime, and we knew if we could hold on for twenty minutes more, we were going to Atlanta. It was almost overwhelming, and we have laughed about this halftime experience many times in our offices at Tech. When we got up to the dressing room area, there was a hallway outside of our assigned space. I was leaning up against the wall in the hall, feeling extremely nauseated and trying to gain some sense of calm before I talked to our team. About that time, Swoopes showed up beside me and began to hyperventilate! My assistants earned every penny that day. They quickly had a paper bag on Sheryl, and kept telling both of us that everything was perfect—we just had to finish! Sheryl and I both got a grip on the situation and were relatively calm when we entered the locker room. At that point, this very special team was able to come together and talk about a blow-out finish for the game.

The second half was pretty much a repeat of the first half. Sheryl put on a show, and our other players followed suit. Our entire bench was up and cheering, and we all began to realize how real going to Atlanta was becoming. I will never forget the feeling I had when it was obvious we were going to win. I was so proud and so thrilled, that I just stood and watched our team, trying to soak in as many memories of those special moments as I could. As Sheryl began to collect her incredible 36 points and 10 rebounds, the crowd began its familiar cheer of *"Swoooooooopes! Swoooooooooopes!"* and the fans in the Big Sky arena watched in awe of her phenomenal performance. We beat Colorado, 79–54. We were going to Atlanta!

Goddess of Victory—Sheryl Swoopes returned to West Texas to play in an exhibition game before competing in the 2004 Olympics in Athens.

We cut down the nets and went to media. It was at this press conference that Krista said what is probably my favorite quote of the year and the one that set the tone for the next week. A reporter asked her what it felt like to play with someone like Sheryl Swoopes. Krista grinned and said, "I have always felt like the best player in the nation should get to play in the *Final Four*, and now she will get to. I'm just really proud for her." The look on Sheryl's face is one that I will never forget. At that moment she knew how much her team-mates loved and supported her, wanting her to get the recognition that she deserved. She also decided that she didn't want to just get there, but she wanted to win it. That became our renewed focus and mission.

People have told me many times that Sheryl Swoopes could have led any team to a national title. My reply has always been the same—yes, she certainly had the talent to do so, but it took a special group of unselfish teammates surrounding her to give her the freedom. There was not another team in America with that combination of a great player and an unselfish team in one package; what they did together was magic, and we all were beginning to believe we really could be champions.

Anyone who has been blessed with the opportunity to compete in a *Final Four* knows what our next week was like. I had ever experienced anything so overwhelmingly wonderful before or since. When we arrived home from Missoula, the airport in Lubbock was packed. We had police lines to help us retrieve our luggage and get to our transportation. Lubbock was ecstatic, to say the least. The city's response to our opportunity was awesome! We worked more hours and tried to deal with more details than I can even remember. Ticket lists, hotel arrangements, phone calls of good luck, media requests, travel for team, families, donors, fans and support groups had to be dealt with so quickly because we were only at home for a couple of days. Obviously, our coaches were glued to video machines and monitors trying to dissect the other three teams and make sure we were ready to prepare our team. And somewhere in between it all, we had to pack and get ready to be on national TV, attend some banquets, and appear at media events. At a time such as this, you'd better have a fantastic staff and a great support group, as well as a diminished need for long periods of sleep! This is where the rewards of building a strong support staff pay off. It was going to take literally everyone to realize the vision begun a decade ago.

Jeannine and I went to Atlanta a day earlier than the team. I wanted to go to the pre-tournament meeting just to get my bearings, because I had never done this before. I also thought that I could concentrate better on getting ready for Vanderbilt away from Lubbock and some of the distractions that were going on there. I laugh when I think back on the day we arrived in Atlanta and picked up one of our courtesy cars. Jeannine was awesome and was trying to deal with everything she possibly could so that I wouldn't have to. We left the hotel to go to the meeting, and when we got in the car, Jeannine said, "Now you don't worry about anything, let me take care of things for you so you can relax and just get ready to coach." I really appreciated that statement and trusted that she would do that. We pulled out of the hotel driveway and immediately found ourselves going down a one-way street the wrong way! We both died laughing. She said in her own choice words, "Well, @#@#! I bet you feel a lot damn safer now, knowing I'm in control!"

The frenzy and chaos continued to surround us. I know that any experience in a *Final Four* atmosphere would be amazing, but having a player like Sheryl Swoopes who captured the imagination and hearts of people all across America made it even more wonderful and overwhelming. Everywhere we went people wanted to have the opportunity to see her, talk to her, and admire her. We had a breakfast for a thousand or so coaches and others who honored her as the National Player of the Year. We also attended a press conference and a banquet for the All-Americans, in addition to the normal press conferences for the practices and games. It would have been easy to lose focus during this week. It makes what Sheryl accomplished even more impressive. One of my favorite moments with her was when we were walking off the stage after she received her Player of the Year honor. A reporter immediately questioned her, asking, "Is this the best award that you have ever received?"

Sheryl's answer touched me forever. She said, "There is no doubt that this is a great honor, and I am really, really proud to be the Player of the Year, but make no mistake: the reason that I came to Atlanta is so that my teammates and I could put National Champion rings on our fingers, and I won't be satisfied until we get that done." To me, the most impressive thing is that she backed it up. Very few times do events or individuals live up to the build-up of great moments. I have to say that Sheryl not only lived up to the hype, but surpassed it each step of the way. She was incredible. People have often asked me what it was like to coach someone like Sheryl, and I have to agree with Swoopes' former South Plains College coach, Lyndon Hardin. He said, "Sheryl was always the kind of player you didn't coach, you just sponsored. Just make sure she's on the bus and tell her what color of uniform to wear." My sentiments exactly.

Vanderbilt was ranked as the best team in the nation the week of the *Final Four*. They were really solid on both ends of the floor. They had a 6'10" post player named Heidi Gillingham and perimeter players who could shoot out the lights from a couple of feet behind the three-point arc. They scared our coaching staff because we were exclusively a zone defensive team, and their combination of an All-American post player and good perimeter shooters was difficult to deal with. If we double-teamed Gillingham, we were susceptible to the perimeter shot; if we played pretty straight up (a true match-up player for player) than we ran the risk of Heidi's shooting skills, her innate talent, and her obvious height advantage. I initially thought we would have to score lots of points in order to have a chance to win. As it turned out, it was a low-scoring game, and we had a great run down the stretch to win. Vandy did not shoot the three-point shot as well as we anticipated against our zone, and our double team defense against Gillingham threw them off. We, on the other hand, didn't get many points off of turnovers or fast breaks. The game basically became a half court, five-on-five slugfest by two heavyweight teams.

In the end, our defense shut the Commodores' shooting percentage down to 35%. Swoopes made 31 points and had 11 rebounds. On one possession, she got three of her own rebounds and then finally put in the shot! She was not to be denied. "*Swooooooopes!*" again resounded through Atlanta's Omni Arena filled with 16,141 women's basketball fans. We finally won the game 60–46 and were going to play for a national championship. We were ecstatic. The walk to the dressing room was something I will never forget. We were so happy, yet so focused on what we had to do the next day. (In 1993 the women's championship was played back to back days for television purposes.)

After we took care of all of the media obligations, we went back out on the floor and watched Ohio State and Iowa play. It was an intriguing match-up. First of all, they were both from the Big 10 Conference, so both teams had already played each other. Second, they had different styles of play and third, both teams were extremely talented and well-coached. It turns out that they played into overtime. When this reality was announced in the Omni Arena, the Texas Tech fans stood up and gave a standing ovation. This overtime was significant for us because we were to play early Sunday afternoon (the next day) for the championship. Ohio State finally prevailed, 73–72. The championship match-up was set.

People often have asked what the hours before the national championship were like. For me, they were some of the most emotional hours of my life. I never slept, and I ran through every part of our game plan a million times during the night. I checked the clock every hour and then would begin thinking about every *what-if* game situation I could think of. Then I would switch gears and wonder about the reactions of people around me when we won. Interestingly, I never thought about losing, but felt an enormous responsibility to win. Not only would this be the first national championship for our program—it would be the first one in any sport for Texas Tech. I felt that very deeply and thought about it much of the night.

One would think the hours before the game would pass slowly, but in reality, that morning was fairly rushed. I got up early, put on my team warm-ups and prepared to go to the arena and walk through our game plan with the team. Before I left, however, I went to Jeannine McHaney's room. I knew that she wasn't feeling well, that the tournament had taken a physical toll on her. Her journey with her disease had been a difficult, up and down series of treatments and surgeries. She had been through chemotherapy earlier and a part of her lung had been removed due to the cancer's spread. That she was even with us in Atlanta and felt like being part of the championship run was at once amazing and humbling to me. Little did I know that after having won many battles, Jeanine would lose the war eighteen months later. I walked in and found her resting on her bed. I told her that this was going to be a great day and that she was responsible for all of the hard stuff it took to get us there. She smiled and nodded her understanding. I told her I would meet her downstairs for the start of the final step of our dream.

When I met the team in the lobby, I looked very closely at the key people to read their moods. I thought that they all looked surprisingly calm and expectantly excited. I desperately wanted to keep them that way. At the arena, we talked through our game plan. We calmly walked through all of the intricacies we thought were important for winning against a very talented Ohio State team. I didn't raise my voice or give any emotional speeches that day. None were needed. These were the overachievers I had depended on all season who wanted more than anything to finish the journey that day.

It is amazing that at that time, we were playing the biggest game in the history of our program, and we didn't even have twenty-four hours to get ready. When the rules changed and the women's games were split with a day in between, it was an excellent improvement in the format that has definitely had an effect on the quality of our championship games. However, in 1993, we were more fortunate than Ohio State. Their turnaround was much shorter than ours.

After our walk-through, we ate our pre-game meal. All year long we had handled our pre-game situation the same. We went to a cafeteria and let our players choose, within reason, what they wanted to eat—what they thought made them feel their best. We did not want to break routine now of all times. It took some time, but my staff did a great job of convincing a cafeteria not far from our hotel to open and serve us lunch items around 10:30 AM. We told them to have fried chicken ready, and they did. That is what almost everyone ate, as if we needed a bit of comfort food to get us through the day.

We went back to the hotel, dressed for the game, and began to gather our thoughts. We were to reconvene in the lobby an hour later. As I have mentioned previously, the time before games is always the toughest for me and, certainly on this day, it was magnified a hundred-fold. I was almost physically sick as I considered the magnitude of what we were about to attempt. My knees became weak again, and I was afraid I wouldn't make it to the bus! At that point, I literally dropped to my knees and asked God to give me the strength to complete this mission—not to win, but to be the best I could be that day. I finally got up with a calmness that I know I couldn't provide for myself. I confidently went to the lobby and began to view all of the chaos and circumstances surrounding the game from a perspective above everything else. I entered the arena with an excitement that I could hardly contain.

I remember driving around the front of the Omni to get to the team entrance ramp and seeing lines of people at every entrance. There were scalpers on the streets, street vendors who had Tech shirts, and all kinds of red and black on every block. It was incredible. We went to our dressing room, and the players were quiet, but seemed to be focused on what we were about to attempt. Three events that I will always treasure took place before we ever went on to the floor. Another part of our pre-game routine all year was for the players to write the goals for that particular game on a board, without the coaches being present. This always helped them to verbalize what was important without our dictating it to them. We usually had about five or six goals dealing with everything from our shooting percentage, to the opponents' shooting percentage, to the number of rebounds we would probably need to win. When I walked into the dressing room after they had finished writing their goals, there was one statement written on the board, and it said it all. "WIN THE WHOLE THING!"

The second memorable moment was when Sheryl Swoopes gathered our three freshmen players around her, knowing that they might not see a lot of the action that day. She looked them straight in the eye and told them that they would have to continuously pray for her during the game and that she could not do it without their help. This, to me, was proof enough of her champion's heart; the wide-eyed freshmen could do nothing but comply and knew they had a part in the day's objective, too.

The third moment and one of my all time favorite memories with my staff occurred right before we all walked onto the floor, just prior to the introductions. I gathered them all into a huddle and told them that I was so glad and honored that we were going to experience this day together. I told

Victory is near!

them how proud I was to be coaching this game with people of their expertise and loyalty. We all hugged and then walked through a curtain that would change us forever.

The championship game was a great one. Ohio State had not even been ranked in the preseason but had made their way to Atlanta. It would be a game pitting two All-Americans and the future of women's professional basketball against each other—senior Sheryl Swoopes for Tech and freshman Katie Smith for Ohio State. Little did they know that eleven years later they would be teammates on the 2004 U. S. Olympic women's basketball team.

Lady Buckeye coach, Nancy Darsch, had been to the *Final Four* before as an assistant with Tennessee, so the atmosphere was familiar to her. The Omni was packed with a sea of red—red and white for the Buckeyes—red and black for Texas Tech. Sitting in the crowd, all the way from Brownfield, was Louise Swoopes, Sheryl's mother, who had taken her first ride on an airplane. When CBS tried to get an interview from her, she declined saying she was too nervous. "Can't Beat Swoopes!" and "Can you Believe Swoopes?" signs appeared throughout the Lady Raider crowd, playing off the CBS logo. The Texas Tech band, the Court Jesters, were into the game as well. One of Ohio State's star players was senior Nikki Keyton, who had sported a red, Betty Rubble-esque bow in her hair during the Iowa game. All of the Court Jesters showed up with red bows in their hair, too. The Lady Raider Nation was ready to play.

The game was a nail-biter from the tip-off. We anticipated that the game

VICTORY!

would be fast-paced from the beginning, and we were right. The intense tempo was fast, with both teams going from end to end, driving, passing, and making incredible plays. Throughout the first half, the score see-sawed back and forth. However, by the middle of the first half, all Swoopes heard was the sound of records falling. She passed the all-time tournament scoring record early in the half and at the 8-minute mark had accumulated the most points scored in a half by an NCAA player. Significant to Swoopes' unbelievable play was the strength of our starting line-up's other members. Ohio State double- and triple-teamed Swoopes which left Kirkland, Scott, Johnson, and Clinger free to score. One of the advantages a great player gives you is this kind of secondhand offense due to unguarded players. Swoopes missed only three shots the first half. We went to the locker room ahead, 40–31.

Following the half, Ohio State came back with renewed energy. Katie Smith proved why she was an All-American and the Women's Basketball Freshman of the Year, making some incredible shots and leading her team to within two points, 54–52. Keyton made a significant field goal and the Lady Buckeyes went ahead for the first time since early in the game, 55–54. It meant so much to me at this point that every member of our team contributed to this win in game-changing ways, as from this point to the end of the game, Swoopes was being guarded by so many Ohio State players. Stephanie Scott, in her signature kneepads, made some incredible dives for balls and defensive plays. Noel Johnson made some crunch shots for us as well as

Sheryl Swoopes and Krista Kirkland Gerlich enjoy a championship reunion memory.

some significant free throws. Cynthia Clinger was a workhorse under the basket, getting rebounds and creating offense of her own. Kirkland and Swoopes reverted back to what had taken them to the *Final Four* in the first place—an intuitive sense of where the other was and what she was going to do with the ball. We were ahead 61–59 when Swoopes began another of her amazing takeover runs. She was 11 for 11 from the free throw line, thanks to drawing fouls from the four Ohio State defenders. With three minutes left in the game, Clinger fouled out, and Lady Raider freshman Michi Atkins from Loraine, Texas, went in as center. The biggest crowd she had played in front of in Loraine was when the high school gym was packed with 150 enthusiastic fans. She accepted the pressure with grace, however, and made offensive and defensive contributions which made a huge difference in the outcome. With the help of Ohio State's Smith, Keyton, and Brucy, the Buckeyes brought the score back to 84–79 at the three-second mark. Then, Stephanie Scott made a huge, diving steal-play, in which Kirkland got fouled. At that point, I was beginning to feel for the first time like we would pull out the win. I sat down between Linden and Roger and hugged their necks, not believing that any of it could actually have happened. Even though Brucy clinched several three-pointers during the last three minutes, we came out with the win, 84–82. Someone had re-fashioned Burger King crowns for us to wear. Seniors Swoopes, Kirkland, and Clinger raised the championship trophy,

Reunion huddle of 1993 champions—United Spirit Arena—January 2003.

symbolizing how much of a team effort this road to the *Final Four* was. Krista voiced our collective small town wonder at accomplishing this amazing feat when she said in a post-game interview, "Who would have thought that a little ol' Spearman girl would be a national champion?"

I later heard from a photographer friend what had happened in Lubbock on Tech's campus when we won. He was stationed by the Texas Tech fountains, close to the entrance to the campus, listening to the game by radio. Following the win, the campus was unusually quiet. He had just decided that his plan to be there for some great photos was not going to pan out. Suddenly, he said, the dormitory doors burst open and students poured out, gathering around the Will Rogers horse, cheering on the grounds, splashing and screaming in the fountains. I've always wished at the moment of our win that I could have been in two places at once.

I have watched the championship game a few times since then, always seeing something new. There were obviously great athletes on both sides who understood their roles and played as hard as they possibly could. In the press conference afterwards, I said nobody took anything back to the dressing room from either side—those players had left everything on the floor, which should define a championship game. For us, nothing has ever been the same. That afternoon, and for a long time afterwards, the emotions and memories our staff shared with our players, administration, families, and fans were indescribable. We

FINDING HER VOICE

COACH WEESE REMEMBERS THE BEGINNINGS OF COACH SHARP'S REPUTATION AS A sought after speaker. The first year at Texas Tech, she was asked to speak at a high school sports banquet in Spade, Texas. The actual banquet was to be held at the K-Bob's Steakhouse in Littlefield, as Spade didn't have a restaurant large enough to accommodate the crowd. Sharp invited Weese to attend the event with her. Weese sensed that Coach Sharp was a nervous wreck and asked what was wrong. She said that speaking engagements were the part of her new job she most feared, that talking in public made her extremely nervous, even to the point of nausea. The two got to K-Bob's, greeted everyone and sat down to dinner. When Coach Sharp was introduced to speak, Weese eyed her uneaten pecan pie, thinking that during the speech he would have time to help himself. About halfway through the pecan pie, Sharp wrapped up her thoughtful, but brief, speech. It had lasted all of about nine minutes. Short and sweet. Little did either of them realize that about eleven years later, she would be standing in the White House Rose Garden speaking to more than 50 governors, senators, and even the President himself after winning the National Championship. More recently, Sharp was invited to speak to members of the U.S. Department of Defense regarding leadership. This is proof of what Sharp encourages her players to do all the time: "If you work on your weaknesses long and hard enough, they will soon become your strengths."

had done what we had set out to do ten years earlier and had realized a dream.

The welcome home our fans gave us when we got back to Lubbock was the perfect ending to the fairy-tale ride. We had been told that there was going to be an event to welcome us, but we never could have imagined what awaited us. Texas Tech and Lubbock city officials had decided to hold the celebration in our football venue, Jones Stadium. We arrived in Lubbock on a commercial airline a little before 8:00 p.m. on Monday night. We were welcomed on the runway and taken back to the campus in limousines. When we went through the ramps into the stadium, policemen on motorcycles surrounded us; I remember thinking how terribly loud their sirens were. However, when we came out of the tunnel, I never heard the sirens again. The roar of the crowd was deafening. 40,000 people had shown up to welcome us and celebrate with us—many waiting three or four hours just to see us arrive. Texas Tech students from all over the country cheered with the small town faithful and soaked in the glory. When Swoopes was introduced, the players, the band, the cheerleaders, the coaches and everyone in the stands started bowing down to her, yelling "*Swoooooopes!*" for one last time, and chanting, "We're not worthy! We're not worthy!" When Krista was asked to speak, I believe she said it best for all of us, "Before now, I'm not sure we knew what we had done, but now we know, and we thank you so much." The 40,000 West Texas well-wishers erupted.

Our team banquet that spring was attended by fourteen-hundred fans. I told them that I didn't expect the greatest event in those young women's lives to have taken place when they were from eighteen to twenty-two years old. I wanted to believe that the championship would lead them to greater moments. Over a decade later, I can honestly say that that has indeed been the case. They have done terrific things with their lives. From lawyers, to stay-at-home moms, to basketball coaches, to educators, to artists, to professional basketball players, to Olympians, these champions have used their experience to wonderfully enhance the communities in which they find themselves. Nothing could make me happier or more proud—but that Sunday in the spring of 1993 is a day we will remember forever.

THE 1993 LADY RAIDER CHAMPIONSHIP TEAM

DIANA KERSEY #13

STEPHANIE SCOTT #20

SHERYL SWOOPES #22

JANICE FARRIS #24

MICHELLE THOMAS #30

MELINDA WHITE #50

NIKKI HEATH #15

KRISTA KIRKLAND #21

NOEL JOHNSON #23

KIM PRUITT #25

CYNTHIA CLINGER #34

MICHI ATKINS #5

5

FAME

1993–1994
Lady Raider Average Home Game Attendance: 7,007

"Unblemish'd let me live, or die unknown;
O grant an honest fame, or grant me none!
ALEXANDER POPE, *The Temple of Fame*

FTER WINNING THE NATIONAL CHAM-
pionship, I rested on our laurels for a
bit, enjoyed the moment, and then
recommitted to discovering new
goals and dreams for our program.
Gratitude for the opportunity to do
what I do is something I continually
felt in the months following the
championship—and continue to feel
today. I am constantly amazed at the
opportunities I have been given and
always want to give my best effort to
Texas Tech, our fans, and certainly my staff and players. I have been incredibly
blessed because I am passionate about basketball and also about young
people. In my life, those two things collide daily to create very special
opportunities for everyone involved.

The positive elements of success are open doors for taking anything
you are associated with to an entirely new level of greatness. If you learn
from success and develop new or stronger goals, you will maintain a consistency that sustains success. As I've said before, the visibility of your program
is never higher than in the wake of a national championship. Using that
visibility to expand your recruiting opportunities, to increase your fan base,
and to multiply donations to the athletics department will take your entire
program to new heights. There is a limited window of opportunity to capi-
talize on this rare accomplishment, so you must gather the forces, have a
plan, and force the action. You cannot do this effectively if you are basking in
the glory of wonderful, but fleeting fame. You must go back to work.

The United Spirit Arena in Lubbock is visible evidence of success and
hard work. Following our championship run, we had to address a very good
problem—accommodating our crowd. The Lubbock Municipal Coliseum
had been our home ever since I had begun coaching. It accommodated
about 8,000 people comfortably. In the mid 1990s, our average crowd began
to hover consistently around that number. We were obviously thrilled with
the increased support, but knew that we needed to address this aging venue
with something Lubbock and West Texas could enjoy for a long time. We
wanted a high quality arena that would be state of the art in terms of a sporting

The United Spirit Arena has room for hot air balloons!

facility as well as a setting for concerts and other community events. The Texas Tech administration took this as a goal and assembled a group of administrators, regents, students, and coaches to research the possibilities and determine a design. Men's basketball coach James Dickey and I were fortunate to have been on that committee. We traveled the country looking at various arenas and finally came up with a design "wish list" important for everyone. Among other things, we wanted most of all an intimate arena where the fans could sit close to the floor and be part of the action. We knew firsthand the crowd's importance to our success; much of the design process was with that in mind. We also wanted the locker rooms, training rooms, offices, seats, and concessions to be first rate, so that coming to watch a Texas Tech basketball game was truly a special event. We wanted our players, as well, to have a sense of pride in their "house" and have the confidence of a great facility to showcase their talent. As we determined a plan, I strongly felt the weight of each design decision, knowing that what we were building would be around long after we were gone. It had to be right. One of my favorite moments was when Coach Dickey and I were asked to go to the arena and see if the seats were the right color. We knew we wanted Red Raider red, but also knew that given the light, the seats might resemble A&M maroon or Longhorn burnt-orange. That would never do! We put on our hardhats, went to the arena, and I will never forget Coach Dickey's expression when the arena lights were turned on. He turned to me with a

The Lady Raider locker room—United Spirit Arena.

huge smile and said, "They're red! They really *are* red!" Then we laughed and gave each other a high five.

As it turns out, the reality of the United Spirit Arena has surpassed all of our dreams. Not only do our fans have a great place to watch a basketball game, with the closest seats no more than twelve feet from the out-of-bounds line, they can also enjoy an atmosphere unequaled in women's basketball. Believe me, when we were scheduled to play the opening game in the arena, I was really concerned that we would be unable to fill up our new 15,000 seat venue. Could we really double the number of fans that had shown up at the Coliseum? We had scheduled a tournament to celebrate the opening—the *Four in the Fall Classic* on November 20, 1999. We were to play Louisiana State University, coached by legendary Hall of Famer Sue Gunter, a pioneer of women's basketball and one of its greatest champions. The crowd was a sell out with 15,050 in attendance! I was ecstatic. Not only did we win that game, 56-49, but the Lubbock community and Texas Tech had stepped up to the plate to show what a united spirit could produce. Our success in 1993 was paving the way for bigger and better accomplishments, and today I continue to be humbled by the embrace of our fans, our administration, and the West Texas community. In my book, the arena is the best place in the country to watch a basketball game!

And so it follows that perhaps the most important precept to be gleaned from success is gratitude. One of the biggest lessons we can teach

Fans enjoy Marsha Sharp Day at the United Spirit Arena following Sharp's 500th win.

the young women in our program is to acknowledge acts of kindness from other people. The outpouring of shared happiness and affirmation for our program was unbelievable following our championship run. We truly began to be treated like royalty, and it became important to me to make sure our players were gracious winners. It has been particularly distressing to me throughout the years that so many kids reach an age of accountability and don't know how to write thank you notes! Unfortunately, too many people believe that their fellow human beings owe them acts of kindness. That mentality is one of my pet peeves! In our program at Tech, the coaching staff tries to instill gratitude in our players and demonstrate it ourselves. Some of my favorite things to receive from former players are thank-you notes for a media guide, an invitation, or something else we have tried to do to keep them engaged. When a Lady Raider feels confident in expressing gratitude, I know that we have helped her develop a lifetime skill that will serve her well long after she leaves our locker rooms. I was so proud of Sheryl Swoopes and the other members of the 2004 USA Olympic basketball team after their gold medal run in Athens. In every interview, they were gracious winners, not only toward the other members of their team, but also toward everyone who had helped them get there, including those they defeated. That gratitude is one reason they endeared themselves to the American public and to the world at large. Because of their graciousness in victory, they will continue to enhance the rise of women's basketball for many years to come.

OH, I WISH THAT I COULD BE A HALL OF FAMER

HOW DO YOU RECOGNIZE A HALL OF Famer? That was a question on the minds of many who were invited to attend the 2003 Induction Gala Ceremony for the Women's Hall of Fame in Knoxville, Tennessee. The names added to the list that year were these: Tara Heiss (player, University of Maryland), Leon Barmore (coach, Louisana Tech Lady Techsters), Claude Hutcherson (fan-pilot-benefactor, Wayland Flying Queens), Patsy Neal (player, Wayland Flying Queens), Doris Rogers (Nashville Business College), Marsha Sharp (coach, Texas Tech University Lady Raiders). Is it in their eyes? Is it in the way they handle a ball? Is it in the way they carry themselves down the street? Is it in the way they inspire folks to be their best? What exactly is it? The answer isn't simple, but one thing is for sure—while each Hall of Famer stands alone on a formidable stack of impressive statistics and on the historical shoulders of those of the same ilk, they all seem to share this in common—intensity. There is an other-worldly electricity about them, a presence, that fills a room, and all of a

sudden, you feel like you, too, can accomplish anything.

Witnessing an induction ceremony is truly a singular experience. Imagine a room full of basketball coaches and players, present and past. Hall of Fame basketball players are spotted easily enough, their heads rising above the crowd like graceful giraffes. The coaches, however, are obviously sometimes shorter and a bit trickier to spot. Regardless of their journeys, though, their intense passion is everything. Like painters love the smell of paint, like baseball players love walking on freshly clipped grass clenching a new glove, these inductees are helplessly addicted to speed, finesse, strategy, the feel of the ball, and most of all, finding a way to win. Being named a Hall of Famer is important to them, but it is also just affirmation of what they cannot help but do.

The evening itself was all about honoring the past, celebrating the present, and promoting the future of women's basketball. Former inductees participated in a kind of roll call of greatness, being introduced on stage and vocalizing a quote that had inspired them to greatness. Some invoked Eleanor Roosevelt, Helen Keller and even Mark Twain while Flying Queens coach Harley Redin offered this simple, raspy, West Texas twanged reminder— "Fundamentals win ball games." He spoke it with passionate conviction, as if it were nothing less than God's truth.

One moment, from a player's standpoint, spoke volumes about this mysterious, shared intensity. Sixty-two year old inductee Patsy Neal played for the Wayland Flying Queens from 1956–1960, where she assisted in their

Marsha Sharp and Flying Queen All-American Betty Cagle
at the Women's Basketball Hall of Fame.

winning two AAU national titles. She also was a three-time All-American and has the distinction of winning the National Free Throw Title in the 1957 AAU National Tournament. At that contest, she nailed 48 of 50 free throws! Following her gracious acceptance speech on the stage of Knoxville's Tennessee Theatre, she called offstage to the wings. A larger than life blue ball spangled with stars was bounce-passed gracefully to her. Neal gleefully twirled it high on one finger to the audience's delight. Then she hoisted her twenty-five pound bronze award with one hand in deference to the crowd's vigorous applause and briskly exited the stage. What passion, this?

Coach Sharp exhibited the most ardor from a coaching standpoint. The intensity was the same, but it was aimed in another direction. While a player's passion is borne of a recognition of her own talent and joy in playing, the coach's zeal is directed toward recognizing the gifts of others. In Sharp's typical

graciousness, she pointed from the stage to a section in the audience where there were assembled over forty of the Lady Raider faithful. Fellow coaches, former players and family were seated there having just given Sharp a standing ovation. She remembered her parents' encouragement of her dreams and spoke of her family's lifelong support. She named her coaches and assistants as loyal aides along the journey, and especially thanked Linden Weese, for being her sidekick for twenty-plus years. She thanked the Texas Tech administrators for providing the means for getting the entourage there and praised the foresight of the late Jeannine McHaney for encouraging the value of women's collegiate athletics early on. As she mentioned each by name, there was not one who wouldn't have walked over hot coals to be there for her at the moment. Sharp spoke of her humble walk through the Hall of Fame and how she was truly overwhelmed at the

*(Top) University of Texas coach and Hall of Famer Jody Conradt was on hand for
Coach Sharp's 2003 Induction into the Hall of Fame. (Above) Lady Raider Team physician
Dr. Rebecca Raedecke poses with her family at Coach Sharp's Hall of Fame Induction.*

company of greatness to which she had
been named. Former coaches, heroes,
and respected competitors stared back
at her there, and she couldn't believe
she was part of the group she so
esteemed. She mentioned, too, with a
passion that no one missed, that the
Hall of Fame award was certainly not

Sharing the pride of Coach Sharp's Hall of Fame induction was a family affair—Bradley

Martin, Paul Martin, Pam Sharp Martin, Jeremy Martin, Michael Sharp,

Mary Dell Sharp, Jonathan Sharp, Coach Sharp, Emily Foreman Sharp, and David Sharp.

an award for her alone. "This award is an award for Texas Tech University and the whole Lady Raider program. It would be incredibly misplaced of me to put this spotlight entirely on one individual's accomplishment." Spoken like a true coach, this award for her was in every way a team win. That's why her bronze award stands today in the Lady Raider office rather than in a trophy case in her home.

There is something different about these Hall of Famers. They have been that "somewhere in between" of which Texas Tech Chancellor David Smith spoke so eloquently during Coach Sharp's introduction. That place between knowing in your solitude what can be achieved and what hard, hard work must be done to get there. They have learned which battles to fight and which ones to save for other days when it comes to gender equity in women's sports.

What is common, though, in the eyes of any Hall of Famer is also their love of the game and their shared belief that games can be vehicles for dreams. Anyone who attended the induction weekend could not help but come away with a sense of gratitude for games themselves, for healthy rivalries, for fair competition. The idea of sport is a great gift from a Creator kind enough to inspire his creation to play and who must delight also in its beautiful, heart-stopping moments. But this Creator knows, too, that by participating in games, the players find metaphors for how to live. Such perseverance, such commitment, such high, high aspirations, such love of the game, such appreciation for life, family, and friends and such doing of it each and every day. That's how you recognize a Hall of Famer. And that's how you win ball games.

2003 Women's Basketball Hall of Fame Inductees—Leon Barmore, Wilda Hutcherson Redin,
Doris Rogers, Marsha Sharp, Patsy Neal, and Tara Heiss.

When you are blessed with such great talent or immense opportunity, you have a very direct responsibility to give back. There are many ways to do that, but one is to give confidence to as many people as possible. I continually encourage our team to be involved in the community, and particularly with kids, to help them understand the great possibilities in their lives. After 1993, I was dumbfounded by the increased size of the platform a national title provides. We were instantly in a unique position to capture the attention of many different groups. Using our fame to talk to groups about things much more important than dribbling a basketball has come to be one of the most rewarding experiences of my career. Our coaches and players continue to make many appearances at schools to talk to students about drugs, alcohol, staying in school, and accomplishing dreams. Fundraising for the greater good also became a way for us to make a difference. Opportunities such as signing basketballs to be auctioned for the American Cancer Society, Habitat for Humanity, or for the Children's Miracle Network gave each individual player the realization that a national championship was a springboard to more far-reaching endeavors, rather than an end in itself.

As positive as the by-products of a championship season can be, however, I am a firm believer that success can be as destructive as adversity

Finding a way to win characterizes every Hall of Famer.

SOCKS AND THE WHITE HOUSE

ONE OF THE ACCOMPANYING PERKS OF WINNING A NATIONAL CHAMPIONSHIP WAS the opportunity to go to the White House and receive the nation's congratulations from President Clinton. While waiting on the White House lawn, Stephanie Scott saw Socks, the Clintons' cat, saunter around the corner. Not thinking about where she was, she immediately bent down and began to entice the cat to come play with her. When Socks came closer to her, Secret Service men poured out of the bushes, the trees, and the very woodwork it seemed to make sure Stephanie was not going to terrorize, or perhaps kidnap, the Clintons' cat. Needless to say, that at that point, it wasn't the cat who was nervous.

if given the chance. At that wonderful moment of victory in 1993, many people had to make decisions about how that extraordinary experience would affect them. Two of the most dangerous offshoots we faced were complacency and over-confidence.

Complacency is the easiest trap to fall into. There is a tendency for everyone surrounding you to make you bigger, brighter, and better than you really are when you win at a high level. It is a major temptation to fall into the pit of listening to all of your press reports and to all of the positives on television and talk shows and every other form of media. Everyone you see on the street, anytime you go to a restaurant, anywhere you happen to be, wants to share great memories of the year with you. If you don't have some balance, and if you don't immediately refocus on the future, you can lose the structure of your program in a hurry. I am definitely not saying that you should not enjoy the moment and the accomplishments of your team. At the same time, however, you cannot afford laxity in getting ready to compete again. You don't want to be labeled as a one-time success or a flash-in-the-pan program. You want to be in it for the long haul. Walter Winchell was right when he said, "Nothing recedes like success." Don't let complacency be a by-product of your successful season—let your laurels be not only your crown, but your spur to even greater heights.

Over-confidence, however, can be the most destructive by-product of success. Arrogance displayed at the time of one's greatest achievement always lessens the achievement! There is such a difference between, for instance, the Olympian who wins with joy and the one who taunts the crowd, strutting his stuff. If you have made it to the Olympics, we know how good you are! One of the most interesting things I have watched during my career is how success can change certain people. I have to say that some are much better individuals when they are on the journey to success, rather than when they actually experience their "fifteen minutes of fame." All of a sudden, they become totally different people. Their goals, their interactions with others, their mission seems to be affected and, many times, all of their relationships with people around them are damaged. Not only is this attitude common among some of our nation's top athletes, it is tainting the businesses of America as well. Too many corporate magnates have learned how to make it to the top, but have forgotten how to behave when they got there. We must guard against this kind of ethical demise at all costs. I hope that when you sit and dream of that moment when you have a great win or when you reach the top, you also give some thought to how you are going to conduct yourself. You do not want to become someone you don't even recognize because of a special, but fleeting, accomplishment.

The key, then, is to strive always for success, but when it comes, remember to go forward with gratitude, using the experience of your success to make the world a better place. This responsibility is incumbent upon anyone who calls himself or herself a leader of any stripe—coach, CEO, parent, teacher, etc. Moments like the ones we experienced in the 1993 season are rare, indeed. But, they are always reachable and are always beckoning with each season's beginning, leading us to dream greater dreams. Emerson's familiar words say it all. Read them slowly and ponder what your successes can do to make a difference in your world:

"To laugh often and much; to win the respect of intelligent people and the affection of children; to earn the appreciation of honest critics and endure the betrayal of false friends; to appreciate beauty, to find the best in others; to leave the world a little better; whether by a healthy child, a garden patch or a redeemed social condition; to know even one life has breathed easier because you have lived. This is the meaning of success."

ADVERSITY

1994–1995
Lady Raider Average Home Game Attendance: 7,386

Winning is wonderful in every aspect,
but the darker music of loss resonates on deeper, richer planes...
Loss is a fiercer, more uncompromising teacher,
coldhearted but clear-eyed in its understanding that life is
more dilemma than game, and more trial than free pass.

PAT CONROY, *My Losing Season*

Adversity causes some men to break; others to break records.

WILLIAM WARD

CCORDING TO THE OLD ADAGE, IT IS NOT a matter of if an organization will face adversity, but rather how that organization will handle adversity when it inevitably comes. No matter how strong the group, how far-reaching the vision, how marvelous the talent, how impenetrable the chemistry, or how great the success, no team is immune to strife. A coach's ability to handle adversity is one of the most important skills needed for a team to survive. When things are going well, it is relatively easy for a coach to lead. However, leaders must lead during the tough times, too. If my career has taught me anything, it is that a team who handles hardship in a positive fashion can become great, while teams who don't will go the other direction. Therefore, as a coach, I must remember to view difficulty as an opportunity rather than an obstacle. History points to countless individuals, organizations, and nations that became much stronger and confident because they faced and handled adversity. People continue to define themselves by walking through hardships every day. These are the folks who have gone through the fire and come out on the other side different, and usually, better persons. The question for each of us is will the difference be positive or negative?

Nothing builds character in an individual or a team quicker than handling adversity. However, in every instance, difficulty reveals existing character. Coaches will learn the most about their players by observing how they deal with problems and obstacles because these issues will reveal how the players are likely to react in challenging game situations.

The question, then, is how does a leader or coach come up with a plan to handle tough times? Certainly difficult scenarios may develop within any team. When trouble strikes, a good leader will not reach any conclusions without gathering input from as many sources as possible. She will not be afraid to ask the hard questions in order to get the facts, interviewing the individuals directly involved in the problem. And most importantly, she will maintain an objective view for all sides involved, even to the point of seeking outside advice if necessary. If something needs to be fixed, we should go to

Game time at the United Spirit Arena.

the appropriate place to get it repaired, whether it's a broken arm or a broken spirit. The idea that seeking professional counseling or mediation is a sign of weakness is extremely short-sighted.

To have the kind of trust that will allow a player to lean on a coach's decisions, a strong relationship must be in place between the coach and individual team members. And this is another potential problem area. Because the coaching staff demands a high level of performance from the team, it is sometimes frustrating for players. At the same time, the coach may be frustrated because of what is perceived to be a lack of concentration or effort. Or perhaps the player has an attitude that is detrimental to the group. Again, as painful as it may be for both sides, there must be openness and a desire to gather as much information as possible to try to tackle the problem.

Secondly, once a leader has gathered the important information, it is critical that dialogue occur. You must have an open line of communication which allows everyone involved to be a part of the solution. Sometimes this could be the most difficult part, for not everyone will come out on top. It is a great opportunity for you as a coach to find out which individuals are interested in being part of the solution or, more unfortunately, you may discover that some people are actually comfortable in the problem and are not interested in fixing it. I am always amazed by this dynamic, but the longer I coach, the more I realize it is a reality. Making sure that teammates understand each other is crucial to surviving this kind of adversity.

A LESSON IN LEADERSHIP

Plenette Pierson

FORWARD

1999-2003

Kingwood, Texas

WHEN PLENETTE PIERSON WAS GROWING up in Kingwood, Texas, the WNBA was only a wistful dream in the minds of promising female athletes. There was no highly visible professional arena for female basketball players to aspire to when they finished their college careers, unless they coached college teams. So, as a little girl, Plenette told her mother, "You just watch, Mom, I'm going to be the first woman in the NBA!"

When she began her rookie season with the Phoenix Mercury in 2003, that childish boast sprang immediately to her mind as she stepped out on the court. This was it—the intersection of dream and reality—and she was scared to death. It was May 22, 2003, and the Mercury was playing one of its first regular season games against Sacramento. Plenette recalls, "I'm normally never nervous before a game; I just go out there and do what I have to do. But this time, Coach looked down at me, and said, 'Pierson, you're in.' I froze. I kept saying to myself, 'I can't do this, I can't do this.'"

And with that moment, Plenette began to earn her way back to the bench. Simple lay-ups refused to go in; instead they went over the backboard, behind the backboard, off the rim, everywhere but into the net. Sacramento star, Yolanda Griffith, scored 27 points and collected 11 rebounds, earning the best stats for the Monarchs that game. "I was supposed to be guarding her," Plenette says, smiling and shaking her head. "I lost my starting spot, but I was fine. I realized I needed to sit on the bench and learn from the veterans." Pierson ended her rookie year with a game-high 26 points against the Los Angeles Sparks, the team that would later play the red-hot Detroit Shock in the 2003 WNBA championship game. Not bad for a rookie determined to realize her dream.

Unfortunately, earning her way back to the bench was nothing new for Pierson. She had done it once before as a Texas Tech Lady Raider. Coach Sharp's team had just begun the 2001 season, Plenette's junior year. The entire Lady Raider Nation was looking forward to a stellar season with Plenette at post and a variety of weapons on the perimeter, not the least of which was Natalie Ritchie's wicked three-point shot. However, the Lady Raiders had to travel to New Mexico to play the Lobos late in November. Texas Tech lost that contest by just nine points, 65–74. Due to the inhospitable circumstances that seemed to surround every New Mexico game, the Lady Raiders decided to ride home by bus immediately, rather than stay in Albuquerque. Needless to say, the mood was somber and quiet on the way home as team members and coaches pondered what they could have done differently, until Plenette started laughing out loud with someone on her cell phone. Coach Sharp, not liking her insensitivity to the mood of the team and the sobering reality of the loss, made her way to the back of the bus and indicated that Plenette should get off the phone and be quiet. "Nothing had gone in for me against New Mexico," Pierson recalls. "I was frustrated with myself, and so I just started mouthing off to Coach Sharp right in front of the whole team. I was really angry and spewed off all kinds of things to her in a really bad tone of voice. And I regret everything I said to this day." Sharp was keenly aware of Pierson's highly competitive nature and explosive personality, and surmised that if they had been in a one-on-one situation, the problem might have been quickly diffused. However, the entire team held their breath to hear what Coach Sharp would say to her star post-player with the rest of a promising season on the line. Would Plenette really get away with that? Sharp made her decision. Junior Plenette Pierson, the Big 12 Freshman of the Year and Tech's starting center, was suspended from play for the season. No room for discussion.

Back in Lubbock, fans were stunned by the sudden turn of events. Plenette had disappeared from the bench at games. Coach Sharp told her upon their return to the gym that anything Tech had promised Plenette meant nothing now. If she wanted to, she could earn her way back on the team, but it would mean sitting out for this season. Initially, Plenette thought she would just transfer but knew that NCAA rules did not allow transfers to play their first season. She would have lost two years of playing time instead of just one. Her mother also reminded her that, while it was Plenette's decision,

she shouldn't leave a place on negative terms. Plenette decided to stay at Tech. The agreement was that she would have individual practices with then assistant coach, Lance White, and not work out with the team all year. In addition to going to classes, she would also attend counseling sessions for anger management. Coach Sharp would have very little contact with her. Plenette agreed and began a journey through adversity for which she would be forever grateful. "I distanced myself from the team for a while and didn't really talk to them. I knew I needed to work on myself. Then I worked my way back into my relationships with them. When I came back, everyone accepted me."

The Lady Raiders ended the 2001–2002 season with eight wins and eight losses, not at all what the year had promised, but remarkable in that other players like rookie post, Cisti Greenwalt, got some invaluable experience she never would have dreamed of getting her freshman year.

Upon Plenette's return for the 2002–2003 season, the fans sensed a renewed focus, confidence, and energy emanating from the Lady Raiders, especially in the post position. In the back of everyone's mind was the possibility that a return trip to the *Final Four* in Atlanta ten years later might just be the thing to do. In January, the current Lady Raider team listened as the 1993 Championship Team gathered for a reunion, reminding their legacy of what it took to be champions. The Lady Raider Nation watched as Plenette played 1,000 minutes on the season, averaged 17.8 points and 6.9 rebounds per game. The team made its way back to the *Sweet Sixteen* to play Duke in, of all places, Albuquerque, New Mexico, where Plenette's troubled journey had begun. Houston Comets star Sheryl Swoopes called the team before the Duke game to encourage them to do

(Above) Plenette Pierson finishes a lay-up against Baylor. (Right) Playing for the WNBA's Phoenix Mercury fulfilled a dream for Plenette Pierson.

what it took to get back to the *Final Four*. She told them to leave nothing on the bench, but to leave everything on the floor. As if she were heeding the call, Plenette realized her own potential as a leader. "I didn't really know I could be a leader, but I got hurt during the Duke game and strained my groin muscle. I wouldn't let them give me cortisone. I just told them to wrap me up really tight, so I could get back in there and try to win." Pierson ended up playing 37 minutes, making 17 rebounds, and scoring 17 points. However, it wasn't enough that night to overcome the Blue Devils. The Lady Raiders lost 51–57. Plenette's senior season was over. "Coach Sharp wanted so much to take us to the *Final Four*, but I wanted so much to take *her* back to the *Final Four*. She deserved to do that more than anyone. I wish I had it to do over again for her."

In the late spring of 2003, Plenette went on to become the fourth draft pick in the first round of the WNBA draft. Along the way, she learned the hard lessons of self-imposed adversity and received the grace of another chance. Plenette now sees her time away from the team as a gift gleaned from difficulty. "I learned through this that I was willing to do anything in order to play and stay on the team. I also learned how to channel my anger into something positive, like playing better defense or offense, and not just snapping off at somebody. I think I learned from Coach Sharp, too, what it takes to be a leader. I can see now, playing for the Phoenix Mercury, the kind of player I need to follow, who the leaders are, and then try to figure out when I need to be the leader, too. I realized, after leaving Tech, the tremendous amount of leadership Coach Sharp provided in that situation. I just couldn't understand it while I was there. I appreciate everything she did for me; I never would have made it to the WNBA without her."

Pierson returned to Tech following her first professional season to help new Lady Raiders realize their dreams, too, before she headed to Tel Aviv to play basketball for six months. "I could come back here for the next ten years and never repay Coach Sharp enough for what she did for me. I like giving back to them, maybe providing a visible picture of what being a Lady Raider can lead to professionally. Swoopes doesn't have time," Pierson says with a grin and a wink. "But maybe I can give them someone to chase during workouts."

Creativity is often an excellent way to deal with such issues. Sometimes doing something a little out of character or unexpected can really help a situation. For instance, humor might relieve a very tense moment or an unexpected response will perhaps refocus the group. Don't be afraid to go out on a limb and do something different! This is not a new theory, but it is one that works. Abraham Lincoln understood the importance of doing the unexpected in relationships when he said, "Do I not conquer my enemy by making him my friend?" Christ himself admonishes his followers to do the unexpected act, to love one's enemies and pray for one's persecutors. Try the unexpected when you've reached the end of your rope in handling a situation—you might be surprised at the results!

Unfortunately, there is always the temptation to ignore adversity, to delay dealing with it, or worse yet, rush to an answer so that it will disappear. These temptations must be avoided if you want a permanent solution which will actually make your team better. There have been many times when I have thought, "If I just wait, it might go away." But my experience is that seldom does that happen, and besides, you might miss a golden opportunity to make your team stronger. If you are coaching for the right reasons, you don't want any patch jobs—those usually come back to haunt you. You want to get to the root of the problem and spend as much time and as many resources as necessary to truly fix the problem.

A perfect example of this occurred following a 1998 NCAA investigation. The investigation concerned the establishment of athlete eligibility and our distribution of athletic aid. The issues dealt entirely with our compliance; academic staff and coaches were gradually finding out that the individuals whom we had trusted to handle all of our eligibility issues had dropped the ball. Players had been certified by Texas Tech's academic staff, but were not in the proper degree program. The NCAA stipulates that players on scholarship cannot change their majors in midstream, that all hours taken must be toward that player's degree. It is a good rule, but one that must be carefully monitored by any university's academic staff. Unfortunately, Texas Tech had miscalculations in almost every major sport. Not a single coach was involved; however, every athletic program would suffer and most would receive a penalty. Some programs were affected more than others and even now, six years later, some are still trying to recover. Women's basketball lost one scholarship for two consecutive years. Sanctions for the other sports had major effects on everyone's programs. Budgets had to be cut to pay for attorney's fees. Donors became distrustful about the way their dollars were being spent. Recruits began to look at Texas Tech with a jaundiced eye. Our

Coach Sharp studies the action from the sideline.

1993 championship title could have even been on the line had the violations been found to be that severe. It was a very stressful, devastating experience for all of us. I thought one of the worst effects was that people around the nation labeled Texas Tech as a university that did not take academics very seriously. We were ridiculed, and we remained a mainstay of negative media attention for several years. This criticism attacked the heart of Lady Raider basketball, as one of the most significant aspects of my program has been the ability to graduate players; we have always taken that responsibility very seriously and are proud of our 99% player graduation rate. I can honestly say, though, that the university has confronted this adversity with courage and has emerged stronger because of it. It has taken the commitment of everyone involved to fix the problem the right way, and I'm proud to say the Texas Tech stepped up to the challenge.

Not only can problems occur beyond the team setting, they can also occur within it. One of the most difficult decisions I ever had to make was in the 2001-2002 season when Plenette Pierson and I had a confrontation following a loss to New Mexico. The Lobos had beaten us 74-61, and we had not played up to our potential at all. Plenette's outburst on the return bus to Lubbock resulted in her sitting out the rest of the season. Our entire program was affected by that difficult, but necessary decision. The best part of Plenette's courageous story came the next year when we faced New Mexico again. The bracket for the NCAA tournament in 2003 was announced on March 16th,

ON RIDING AN ELEPHANT

THE LENGTHS (OR HEIGHTS) TO WHICH A COACH WILL GO TO PROMOTE HER team's profile or bring awareness to a worthy cause often surpass the call of duty. One of the more interesting events in which Coach Sharp participated was a circus. Her job was to ride an elephant around an arena. Growing up in West Texas does not afford too many elephant riding opportunities, so she had zero experience. She walked up to the elephant in question and couldn't believe she was about to take a ride on such an imposing animal. Sharp barely came up to the beast's knee! She asked the attendant how she was supposed to get in the driver's seat. The attendant indicated his interlocked hands and before she knew it, she was literally launched to the top of biggest animal in the place. Boom! She landed on the elephant's broad back, her legs splayed straight out on either side. The lesson Coach Sharp learned that day? Short folks aren't meant to ride elephants.

and we were to host two games in Lubbock to get things started. If we were fortunate enough to win at home, we would go on to the Midwest Regional in Albuquerque, New Mexico and play again in "The Pit", where our trial had begun the year before.

We beat two very good teams, Southwest Missouri and UC Santa Barbara, in the sub-regional in Lubbock. The University of New Mexico had also played extremely well in the sub-regional in Albuquerque and beat a very strong Mississippi State team to make it to the first *Sweet Sixteen* appearance in UNM women's team history. The stage was set. New Mexico played on Sunday night to qualify, and we didn't play until Monday night in Lubbock. That became significant because the fans in Albuquerque had an opportunity to buy tickets for the regional before we knew whether we were going. By the time we qualified, the game was a sell-out.

I tried to be very honest with our team about what was waiting for us. In addition to overcoming difficult memories, which had completely altered our previous season, our players had to deal with the atmosphere of the New Mexico venue. The arena is aptly named "The Pit", as it can be "the pits" to play there! New Mexico fans have always been extremely rabid. They were especially upset that season because one of our post players, Cisti Greenwalt, had chosen to attend Tech instead of New Mexico. They took the liberty of yelling all kinds of profane things at one of their own. The athletic staff made absolutely no accommodation for anyone from Texas, especially anyone sporting Texas Tech paraphernalia. Our fans' cars were scratched with keys and shoe-polished with obscenities. Going into local convenience stores, Tech fans were booed and sometimes accosted by Lobo aficionados. Even the locker rooms were completely unprepared, containing nothing for the players to drink. Unbelievably, we had to come up with our own toilet paper! I completely understand the passions generated by the home team, but am always disappointed when fans on either side go over the line. The spirit of sportsmanship was definitely absent from this contest, and I knew that our mental state going into this game would make the difference in a win or loss. We talked daily about the challenge in front of us. Every single person making the trip with us was going to have to step up and perform with courage.

The night of our first game, Duke and Georgia played the opening contest. My staff and I went earlier than the team to scout that game. I had already made the decision that when our team arrived, they should come out into the arena and watch a few minutes of the Duke and Georgia game. In hindsight, I am really glad we did that. As soon as Texas Tech appeared in the tunnel, the entire arena began booing them. I think it actually distracted the two teams playing for just a few seconds. The good news was that we got that over with, and our team could sit there for a few minutes and absorb the scene. I could tell by their faces that they were angry, but not intimated by what they saw. We had spoken at length about taking the "loud out of the crowd" and not letting "The Pit" intimidate anything about our game. 16,182 fans showed up for the contest. We came out like gangbusters. It was as if our players converted all the negative cheering into positive energy. By halftime, we were ahead, 41–19. We excelled in terms of turnovers, steals, and shooting percentages. I was absolutely thrilled at how our entire team handled themselves that evening. Cisti Greenwalt, especially, played with grace under pressure, as if she had a mission of her own against her home state. We won the game, 71–48. We were one step closer to the *Final Four*, and we had a lot of individuals stepping up and performing. I was so proud of Plenette Pierson's performance and leadership. She played 36 intense minutes, and made 16 of our 71 points. The players had come together as a team. One of the best things about it was they had learned the value of giving a person a second chance. Plenette and our team had emerged from a difficult year stronger than ever. That win against New Mexico will go down as one of my all time favorites because we won more than just a game.

The win against New Mexico meant that we were among the eight best teams in the country. Duke had beaten Georgia, so we were to play Duke in the *Elite Eight*. If anything, the crowd and surroundings were even worse. The New Mexico fans were out in force, as well, and had become frenzied

Blue Devil fans overnight. The Texas Tech Lady Raider Nation showed up, too, sporting even more red and black than usual. Our cheerleaders had brought mini megaphones from Lubbock to counter the Lobos' deafening noise. Some of the fans had even purchased red and black necklaces made out of New Mexican corn kernels to wear to the game! I thought we handled the atmosphere well again and played well enough to nearly win. At halftime, we were only 5 points behind. The Blue Devils came back after halftime, unfortunately, smelling a trip to the *Final Four*. They had 12 blocked shots to our 3 and made significantly more of their free-throws. I was particularly impressed with Plenette who, after a thigh injury, insisted on getting taped and going back on the court. She had something to prove, and I wanted to give her every chance to do that. In the end, however, Duke beat us, 57–51. Duke's All-American, Alayna Beard had made 28 of their 57 points. The game came down to a couple of critical possessions in the last two minutes. Duke made the big plays when they had to, and unfortunately, we weren't able to get it done. However, I was not disappointed in the mentality we showed in Albuquerque. We handled a very difficult assignment in an exceptionally positive way. I was disappointed, though, that we did not get to go to the *Final Four* in Atlanta 2003, to claim another championship exactly a decade later.

We are all better for having endured the adversity of those two seasons together, and I have never regretted making that difficult, but necessary, decision. I will always have a great deal of respect for Plenette for staying at Tech and getting the help she needed, not only to succeed on the team, but to succeed in life. That she is pursuing her dream of playing in the WNBA is a testament to her passion, competitiveness, and talent. I am one of her biggest fans and am grateful for the lessons we both learned that difficult season.

While a leader has to be committed to the team, times that are difficult to bear will inevitably come in one's personal life. In those times, leaders need to know that your personal life should be the priority and the question becomes how to balance that crisis with your job. Be true to yourself during those times. A great support group combined with a strong faith are required for the particularly complex challenges. When my family went through the extended illness and death of my father, Charles Sharp, both of those factors brought me the most peace and strength.

My dad was one of the most competitive, high-spirited individuals I have ever known. He loved athletics, was a good athlete himself, and could have been a great coach. He also was a very compassionate person, and he always tried to defend the underdog. As a banker, he was in the

Coach Sharp's parents, Mary Dell and Charles Sharp, congratulate
their daughter after the 1993 Championship win.

business of helping people better their lives. In the last few years, numerous individuals have told me how much he helped them by listening to their concerns and financial problems. He was a good man who wanted to be part of the solution.

My parents traveled with our team on many trips, including one to Knoxville, Tennessee, to play in the 1995 NCAA regional tournament. They were there lending their support in any way possible, except that there was something different about the way my dad felt on this trip. I had a strong sense that somehow he wasn't the same and that we were dealing with something that wasn't merely a short-term health concern. Sure enough, during the next year we watched him slowly decline both physically and mentally. It was the beginning of a difficult, agonizing, frustrating, and degrading experience with Alzheimer's disease. Anyone who has ever watched someone they love deteriorate with this disease knows what a nightmare it is for the individual as well as for the family. My mother was an unflagging caregiver and tried to meet his every need. Our whole family was in Lubbock, and we tried to help as much as possible, but my mom sacrificed greatly to take care of him. In October 1998, we finally put my dad in a health-care facility in Lubbock. It was a terrific place where he felt secure and where they took exceptional care of him. I have never done anything as difficult as watching such a vibrant, intelligent man deteriorate

into someone who could not even remember how to walk or even to swallow. I will never forget the emptiness in his eyes or the helplessness in his grip. I tried to visit him every day that I was in Lubbock. It was interesting to realize how his world was reduced to the simplest of pleasures. One of his favorite things was for me to bring him a Frosty™ from Wendy's or a milkshake. That would always bring a smile.

We lost him on July 4th, 1999. I was recruiting at an AAU tournament in Tennessee when I received a call from my brother David that I should probably come home. It was a week before Dad passed away. It was an emotional time when I needed to support my mom and the rest of my family. My friends and my staff were incredible during this crisis, and I was eternally grateful to them for their support. This was also a time when my faith in God was tested and found true. There is no better example for a leader to follow than a God who is concerned with our concerns.

Even though we try our best to avoid it, adversity is certain to be a part of every human experience, whether in team settings or on personal levels. At the end of the day, you as leader must take responsibility for the decisions you make. Sometimes that is the most difficult part, but you must never lose confidence in your ability to lead. There is a surplus of Monday morning coaches and scores of opinions about how decisions should have been made and, sometimes, these critics make good points. However, the important thing is that you took all of the information you could get, you knew the people involved, you were in the situation, and you made the decision you thought was the best at the time. We would all be geniuses if we could make all of our decisions knowing the exact outcome! You must have enough confidence in yourself that you can stand up to second guesses. Instead of fearing adversity, perhaps we should embrace it when it comes, for it will come, and try to learn its difficult lessons. If you must make a hard call, stand strong. You are a leader and leaders should be their best when the going gets tough.

Coach Sharp addresses the crowd.

7

TRADITION

1997–1998
Lady Raider Average Home Game Attendance: 7,946

*It is the ceremony of innocence that the fans pay to see—
not the game or the match or the bout.
but the ritual portrayal of a world in which time stops
and all hope remains plausible . . . .*

LEWIS H. LAPHAM

HERE IS NO QUESTION THAT THE TEXAS Tech Lady Raider fans have separated us from many other women's programs across the country. We have been fortunate that our average game attendance has been among the top five schools in the country for the last decade. Great players love to play in front of great crowds. Our fan base has made it possible for us to attract many high-caliber players to Texas Tech. Recruits and players alike will quickly tell you they were convinced to play here after they watched one of our home games, punctuated by the tremendous atmosphere our fans create. I could never tell you adequately how much gratitude I feel for our loyal supporters or how important they have been to our program over the years.

Connecting the community and the university with your program is imperative to success. As head coach, I see my three most important tasks as recruiting, building relationships with my players, and handling public relations. While I put all of these factors above game plans and workout schedules, I believe the backbone element of those three tasks is maintaining strong public relations. Many coaches have made statements to the effect that public relations were not in their contract. Others demand exorbitant compensation before any talk of meeting the public crosses their screens. Both of these attitudes are definitely dangerous and will eventually cause an athletic program to be so much less than it should be.

Something you must realize is that in today's culture, fans don't just magically appear, especially in women's basketball. Not only is it crucial to have a game plan for winning an actual contest, it is crucial to have a game plan for winning a fan base. The first years I was at Texas Tech, we played in front of about two hundred people a game. We could almost hear each other breathe! It was a long struggle to build that number to a respectable count and then another battle to actually become one of the national leaders in attendance. The first attempts we made at growing the crowds were mostly trial and error. But something we did do right was to try to give everyone a chance to have a personal connection with our players and coaches. Even

Texas Tech High Riders get their guns up.

today, when we might have thirteen thousand people watching us play, there is no substitute for personal connections to fans. If a fan feels like he knows us and has a vested interest in our program, he not only will come to a game, he will also be extremely loyal. We have a committed fan base who sticks with us, even if we are not having a great year. That is the greatest test of incredible fans!

How do you build that kind of die-hard loyalty? One person at a time. You shake people's hands, tell them you appreciate them, talk to them about their importance to the program, and make yourself available. They must have a reason to buy in. The one-on-one contacts we make with people are by far the most important. Whether these contacts are through our coaching staff or through our players is not the issue. The issue is going out of your way to make it happen. To me, this is one of the best parts of my job and an unspoken perk of my job contract. I am genuinely interested in our fans. Many, many of them are my friends with whom I've shared some very special moments in arenas all over this country. What a wonderful experience to create those kinds of lasting memories!

In addition to building relationships one person at a time, you must also have a mindset that you will try anything at least once to find a few fans. No group is too small and no fan is too young for you to speak to. Sometimes you have to come out of your comfort zone to have an opportunity to connect with people. I have ridden elephants, played donkey basketball, kissed pigs, dressed up like a duck, had pies thrown at me, and participated in countless other crazy activities which were definitely out of my comfort zone! But this kind of participation in community events creates a symbiotic relationship: their cause becomes your cause and your cause becomes theirs. One of my favorite stories involves former men's head basketball coach, James Dickey. He and I had been invited to judge a chili cook-off, a huge tradition in West Texas. James is a very classy guy who always dresses well. In all the years he was at Tech, I saw him only a few times when he was not in a suit and tie. He showed up at the chili cook-off, suit and all, and the organizers immediately sat us down in front of numerous bowls of chili ranging from somewhat hot and spicy to ridiculously hot and spicy! James looked at me and said, "Okay, Marsh, tell me what to do because when I take my first bite, it will be the first chili I will have ever eaten." I smiled and immediately asked for more water and crackers on our end of the table. James was definitely out of his comfort zone, but his commitment to community over self made a huge difference that day.

While connecting to the community, those folks beyond the curb, is important, it is also imperative to connect with those in our front yard, the university community—especially its students. This group has always intrigued me. More and more around the country, this demographic is becoming harder and harder to hook, not just for basketball, but for all sports. Our country seems to have developed a generation of cable TV sports fans. People can stay in front of a television set on any given night and watch three or four games, instead of coming to an arena and becoming personally involved. It is a real challenge to connect with students to the point they will become rabid fans. Some schools have accomplished this with specific programs, and I have looked for common elements which have consistently made that happen. Wouldn't we all like to have the "Cameron Crazies" that the Duke men's basketball team enjoys? This university fan base has been especially difficult in women's sports. We have to convince all kinds of people that we have a credible product. And again, it begins with one person at a time until it becomes large enough to be "the thing to do" on campus. Gimmicks help some, but eventually it comes down to being able to connect your players to the pride that students feel when they attend your games. The answers are not easy here, but striving for student support is a worthy goal and a yearly challenge. That said, I do have a great deal of gratitude for the Texas Tech band members, namely the Court Jesters, who have been a tremendous part of our success. Their spirited playing and cheering has done so much to guide the passion of the crowd during our most memorable wins. From wearing bows in their hair, to painting their faces red and black, to playing farewell melodies when opponents foul out, the Court Jesters are an integral part of the Lady Raider basketball experience. They, along with the Texas Tech High Riders and Saddle Tramps continue to be the keepers of our university spirit.

The other group that can quickly take your program to another level is the major donors to your university and its athletic program. In most cases, universities could not operate without their generosity. Men's programs have relied on the help of donors for generations. Convincing these benefactors of the importance of women's sports has been a hard sell; persuading them to include us in the distribution of their generous donations, even harder. But, it is something that we have a responsibility as coaches to pursue. It is imperative that we show these contributors the respect they deserve for all of the help they provide, that we spend as much time as possible educating them about our sports, and that we present them with opportunities to be a part of what we are doing. This is one of the new great frontiers for women's coaches, which can and should take women's sports to a more exciting level of funding and competing. These donors are folks who have worked very hard at what they do and just need the right reasons to become more involved with women' sports. Fortunately, a trend toward this end seems to be developing, especially if coaches have taken the time required to show appreciation for all that their patrons are already doing. Coaches must understand that this relationship building is definitely in our job description. We just need to roll up our sleeves and get with it. If you don't feel confident relating to the public, get help! Talk to fund raisers, go to clinics, talk to coaches who have proven they understand what this is all about. Then watch your program take off.

Many universities call our program at Texas Tech for ideas about marketing and to find out how we drive our attendance. Every once in a while we do something special such as offering tickets at a reduced rate, giving away several thousand T-shirts, or some other incentive. However, most of the time our tickets are full price and because of that, we have been fortunate to be one of the leading revenue-producing women's basketball programs in the nation. Not too many years ago, we actually started making a profit, which we could invest into our program. That was a very proud day for me. Our fans are awesome and that accomplishment would not be possible without their loyalty.

While we don't use gimmicks very often, I don't want to leave the impression that we don't work hard at building attendance. We just come at it from a different angle; it takes a long period of time, in some cases, to see

CREATING FANS FOR LIFE

Dr. Catherine Ronaghan

SURGEON/FAN

1997–2000

Lubbock, Texas

IF ANYONE EVER NEEDED AN EXAMPLE OF an avid Lady Raider fan, look no further than about eleven rows up behind the Lady Raider bench in Lubbock's United Spirit Arena. There you will find Ronaghan Row. Dr. Catherine Ronaghan and her husband Bill Nolan, attend faithfully with their three children, her mother, her partner in surgical practice, and various guests. Not only do they have season tickets and attend road games when possible, the family frequently follows the Lady Raiders on major trips to Hawaii or the Virgin Islands. Undoubtedly, Lady Raider basketball has been a major part of their lives, but Cathy Ronaghan admits that she is an unlikely fan.

Dr. Ronaghan doesn't recall a specific moment when she became a Lady Raider fan. Her passion just naturally evolved, not through watching a game initially, but through what she calls "serendipitous" encounters with Coach Sharp. Ronaghan came to Lubbock in July of 1991 as the city's first female general surgeon. Having graduated from the Texas Tech University Medical School, Cathy continued her training at Sloan-Kettering Hospital in New York before returning to Lubbock. She not only is a well-respected general surgeon both locally and nationally, but also is a leading specialist in breast cancer surgery. Ronaghan remembers hearing about Coach Sharp through faculty conversations when Sharp was asked to speak, and she was intrigued with what she heard. Other connections came through Sharp's involvement in the Susan G. Komen Breast Cancer Foundation and the fact that it was Ronaghan who was the surgeon for Sharp's sister-in-law, Emily, when she was diagnosed with breast cancer. Cathy kept hearing about Coach Sharp, how her major responsibility is to her players, not just as a team but also as individuals. She also liked how Sharp used her teaching position to impact the lives of young women, to encourage ethical behavior, and to demand personal responsibility for their lives and their involvement in the community. After finally meeting Coach Sharp at a conference, Ronaghan came home and told her husband Bill that they were

buying season tickets to Lady Raider games. Bill's response was, "What?!" Cathy knew that Bill didn't even like basketball, that neither of them had ever been fans of any sport, and neither of them had ever played basketball. "I'm sure I couldn't have dealt with the fouls," jokes Ronaghan.

Coach Sharp's reputation appealed to her, but so did the opportunity to support women's athletics. In Ronaghan's experience, women's athletics have always been an underdog on university campuses. Revenue, visibility, and Title IX issues had always been a concern of hers as she had faced similar gender-equity challenges in her surgical profession. All of these became reasons to support what was becoming a Lady Raider machine at the beginning of the 1991–1992 season. As she and her family began to watch, Ronaghan realized how much she enjoyed women's basketball. Going with the 1993 team to Atlanta for the *Final Four* was definitely a lifetime highlight. "To me, women's basketball is so much more interesting to watch than men's. I think it's a cerebral thing. There must be incredible strategy and the team relationships are crucial to setting up plays. I always get nervous when the team is doing some sort of intricate play, taking forever to shoot the ball, and then they shoot with just a few seconds left and swoosh, the basket's made. That's great stuff!"

Perhaps it is her Irish upbringing, but Ronaghan is one-hundred percent supportive of her alma mater's women's athletic program. "Year after year," she recalls, "it's about greater things than winning basketball. That's what hooked me." That is also what has hooked the 300 annual members of the Marsha Sharp Leadership Circle, of which Ronaghan is a founding member. The group monetarily supports women's athletic opportunities through providing scholarships, enhancing recruitment, and funding extra competition.

Watching good things happen with the Lady Raiders on the court is matched only by the good things they do off the court in Ronaghan's opinion. Her children attend Christ the King Catholic School in Lubbock. When the school began a Character Counts program for its students, Coach Sharp suggested that Natalie Ritchie be a featured speaker. Ritchie accepted, and her speech included the admonition to the students to do things for the greater good, which impressed Ronaghan. "Our youth are our salvation," Ronaghan says. "The Lady Raider program sends a message that a person must try every day to do her best and do the right thing, not expecting anything in return. It's about doing something purely, working hard together, playing by the rules. In all my years of watching Lady Raider basketball, I have never seen a player or Coach Sharp take a cheap shot. They adhere to something larger than that. And that's the stuff that can be applied not only to a team, but to your profession, to your family, to all of life."

Win or lose, good seasons or not—one of the chief components of a winning program is to have fans who avidly believe in what you are doing, regardless of box scores, national rankings, or win/loss records. Somehow, the beyond-the-court relationships with fans begin to enhance the on-the-court experiences. Fans become part of the team as well, almost "a sixth man" suited up and ready to take on all kinds of opponents—not only those encountered in a forty-minute basketball game, but also those confronted in the ongoing game of life. And when *that* tradition is born, everybody wins.

many results. We present a number of programs that we hope our fans look forward to and enjoy as much as we enjoy doing them. One of our best ideas is what we call our *Run-n-Gun Session*. After each of our home conference games, a couple of our players and I go back out on the floor, sit on tall stools, and talk to our fans about the game. Then I ask the players a couple of questions about their backgrounds or about their futures. We stay around for a bit and sign autographs, take pictures, and just visit with the fans. It has become a special tradition for Lady Raider basketball, and it helps our fans get to know us better. Sometimes we have as many as two thousand fans in the *Run-n-Gun Session*, so it has proven to be a great opportunity to connect us with lots of people.

My radio show operates with the same principle in mind. I do it live each week, usually somewhere in the arena. We usually have a hundred or so people who show up and ask questions, get souvenirs signed, or most important to me, just come to show their support. They get a little more insight into the Lady Raiders and our program by attending, and I get to know them, one fan at a time.

I am also fortunate to have a weekly television show hosted by the same talented guy who hosts my radio show, Ryan Hyatt. He does the terrific play by play announcing for Lady Raider games, as well. Ryan is a walking encyclopedia when it comes to our program and almost anything else in sports. During this TV show, I want to make sure we offer something that our fans really want to watch. I have learned that people who are interested in women's basketball are usually more inclined to be interested in personal stories and funny incidents that occur off of the floor than they are in statistics and game plans. With that in mind, we try to do a special focus on one of our players each week and let that player relate a funny story or experience. We also use this show to let our fans see our dining hall, study hall, dressing room, training room, and other workout areas, so that hopefully they feel connected with us even when we aren't on the floor.

Staying as accessible as possible to the media is crucial in building support for your program. If the media doesn't show up, call them. Somehow you have to convince them to help you; news people can become some of your program's greatest assets if relationships are intentionally built there. If the media in your area is in large numbers, try to be as fair, helpful, and patient as you can. There is no substitute for the exposure they can give you.

Another idea that can connect you with your fans is to invite them to travel with you, either on a regular basis or on a special trip. We try to take at

Texas Tech has fans of all ages.

DEALING WITH THE AGGIE TRADITION

OF ALL THE PLACES TO PICK UP A LESSON IN HUMILITY, TEXAS A&M IS NOT THE place a Red Raider goes. Unfortunately for Coach Sharp, that is exactly where she learned one of her more difficult lessons–grace under pressure. The Lady Raiders had just won a hard fought battle against the Aggies at the G. Rollie White Coliseum, but it is always a formidable challenge to contend with the 12th Man atmosphere that permeates every part of the Aggie experience. The Aggies had screamed, chanted, swayed, sung, and cussed-anything to find a way to win, all for naught. Reveille, the revered Aggie mascot, had even bitten one Lady Raider on the leg! When Tech complained to A&M authorities, they simply said, "It's part of our tradition."

Coach Sharp, thrilled with her team's victory, couldn't wait to get to the locker room, celebrate with her players, and put A&M in her rearview mirror. However, the gym at College Station was designed so that the opposing team had to diagonally cross the court in order to get to the locker room. Passing by the Aggie Corps band was part of that journey as well. Just as Coach Sharp and Coach Weese were marching by, heads high and exuding both relief at having won and defiance at having to put up with their "tradition," Coach Sharp slipped and fell. Whap! The first things that hit the floor were her shoulder blades. Of course, her legs flew straight up, her high-heeled shoes waving in the air. She was mortified, but unhurt. For one interminable moment, Coach Weese and the entire Aggie band were speechless. Sharp looked up at Weese and after a moment said, "Oh, great." When he saw she was fine, albeit turning eight shades of red, he said, "Get up, you danged drunk!" They laughed all the way to the locker room. Talk about leaving *everything* on the court!

least one high profile trip each year and always accommodate as many fans as possible. The senior basketball players of 2004, for instance, took trips to St. Thomas, Orlando, New York City, Hawaii, and a summer tour to Europe. In each of those situations, we had a package available for our fans to travel with us. They really look forward to the opportunity. And obviously, we love having them there, especially cheering us on in the stands at game time!

A standard for Lady Raider basketball is that every single one of our practices is open for our fans. I know that some coaches have a problem with this; certainly you must do what you are comfortable with, but our fans love this. We have some retired folks who are there every single day; they adore our players, and we feel the same about them. They are unbelievably loyal to us. I also have found this kind of openness to be good for our players. It makes them more comfortable about performing in front of people and takes away some of those early season jitters.

A three-headed Fan of the Game—William Anderson, Jonathan Sharp,
and Charles Greenfield are die-hard (and giggling) Lady Raider fans.

Of course, there are many other opportunities which develop during any given year—from signing autographs at a football game to making an appearance at a charitable fundraiser in your hometown. The most important goal is to be creative and make your players understand how important the connection is between what happens on the court and who is sitting in the crowd cheering for them during the season. Thus, in whatever arena we find ourselves, on or off the court, we have the opportunity to make a fan or to disappoint a fan. It is a great lesson to teach our players: Their behavior does make a difference, whether it's in the classroom or at the mall. Basketball players usually stick out over the crowd anyway, but I want our players to take the responsibility of that privilege to heart. I could ask any athlete who has played in our program, and they would tell you that one of the most special rewards for being a Lady Raider was being the recipient of love and support, win or lose, from a loyal group of fans. After two decades of coaching, watching the fan support increase from around 900 faithful souls to the Lady Raider Nation of over 12,000 folks has been simply the most gratifying affirmation of everything we are about at Lady Raider basketball. My hat is off to the greatest fans in the nation!

LEGACY

2000-2001
Lady Raider Average Home Game Attendance: 12,660

I have never given very much thought to a philosophy of life,
though I have a few ideas that I think are useful to me....One is that you do
whatever comes your way as well as you can....Another is that you think as little as
possible about yourself and as much as possible about others and things that are
interesting....The third is that you get more joy out of giving joy to others and should
put a good deal of thought into the happiness that you are able to give.

ELEANOR ROOSEVELT

"Do all the good you can, by all the means you can, in all the ways you can, in all the places you can, at all the times you can, to all the people you can, as long as you ever can."

JOHN WESLEY

T THE END OF THE DAY, WE ARE ALL TO have been about something; the sooner we figure out what that something is, the better. It is through my faith, my family, my friends, our Lady Raider fans, and our players at Texas Tech that I have come to realize the importance of a person's legacy in this life. For me, this idea involves at least three areas: my professional calling — leaving the land better than I found it; my personal community — making a difference where I have the means and opportunity; my private faith commitment — living for God.

Each of these is mysteriously bound to the other, enhancing the whole legacy when faithfully and intentionally pursued.

MY CALLING: LEAVING THE LAND

TO UNDERSTAND MY BACKGROUND AND MY VALUE SYSTEM, IT IS CRUCIAL TO understand the agrarian culture that is West Texas. So many of our fans, players, and coaches can trace their histories back to a family farm somewhere; they know what hard work it takes daily to keep the land vital during feast or famine. They also understand something that farm families have adhered to for years and years: heritage. In early farming communities, families strove to leave something for the coming generations, to take care of the land well enough so they could leave it to their children and grandchildren. "Leaving the land" is a foreign concept in our modern world. Not only are ranches being redeveloped and family farms being sold or parceled out in order to survive economically; the idea of leaving a physical legacy is diminishing also. This regrettable loss is the impetus behind my desire to give something of value back to Texas Tech. My father always said you should leave a place a little better than you found it. And so, I began to search for my way to leave a legacy and stay true to the philosophy Dad instilled in me and which I try to instill in our players.

I have never assumed to believe I could completely repay Texas Tech

Coach Sharp welcomes the community to the grand opening
of the Marsha Sharp Center for Student Athletes.

for the wonderful opportunities this university has afforded me. Because of my job, I have enjoyed many financial rewards, have been given all of the tools needed to be successful, and have benefited from a wealth of travel experiences. I decided that I would love to return part of this investment to the university and, more specifically, to the athletics department. I began to put much thought into what would most appeal to me in that regard. I made a list of several of the points which were engaging to me and prayerfully considered the right direction to go. I finally decided on this criterion:

- my contribution would have a lasting impact
- this investment would be bigger than anything I could accomplish on my own
- it would impact every athlete at Texas Tech, not just a select few
- it would make a statement.

At the same time I was deliberating this investment in the future of Tech athletics, the university was unfortunately going through the very difficult NCAA investigation you read about in Adversity, Chapter 6. As I mentioned earlier, for me the worst effect was that others began to perceive Texas Tech as a school unconcerned about student athletes' academics. When I actually put all of the facts in front of me, I knew what I wanted to attempt. I went to our athletic director, Gerald Myers, and told him that I wanted to make a $100,000 donation to generate enough attention and support to develop a student athlete academic center. I thought the idea of an academic center met all of my personal criteria and yet made an equally important wide-ranging statement: The athletics department at Texas Tech did indeed care about academics. Gerald and I went to see the Chancellor of the university, John Montford, and the Marsha Sharp Center for Student Athletes was born. We had a number of donors step forward to make the dream a reality; I will be forever grateful to them for their support and generosity. In the spring semester of 2004, the center opened its doors for any student athlete at Tech to receive every component possible to help them to complete their degrees. On ribbon-cutting day, about two-hundred fans, students, and contributors gathered in the cold January wind to see the opening of this state-of-the-art facility. It was especially meaningful to me and my family, as many of the original donations were given in memory of my dad. It was one of the most fulfilling moments in my career, and I was aware that this was something that would live long after I was gone. I could not have been more proud to share it with the Texas Tech athletic family.

This building, for me, is a part of the big picture which should be a consideration for all of us. Texas Tech has been unbelievably generous to me. I have always been grateful for the confidence they have shown in our program and have appreciated our administration's believing in us enough to allow the Lady Raiders to be a financial player. Our fans have played a huge part in this effort. Their willingness to step up and purchase tickets at some of the highest prices in the nation, as well as buying personal seat licenses, which entitle them to the best seats in the house for both women's and men's games, has made this possible. I don't know of another program in the nation which has a PSL program for women's athletics; it has literally added millions of dollars to the debt retirement schedule of our new arena. Lady Raider fans are incredible and have truly caused us to stand out from most other programs in the country. There is no question that I have one of the best jobs in the nation because of them.

I say all of this to emphasize that if this university had not treated women's athletics equitably, there is no way that I could have started the academic center project. Because of the administration's generosity and the loyalty of our fans, the student athletes at Texas Tech will be rewarded. This is the way it should work. I talk to our players all of the time about the biblical directive that much is expected from those who are richly blessed. Hopefully, "leaving the land" through the Marsha Sharp Center for Student Athletes will make a tangible difference in the lives of Texas Tech athletes

In 1995, Coach Sharp welcomed Texas Governor George W. Bush
to the first Komen-Lubbock Race for the Cure.

for years to come and stand as a testament to one of the Lady Raider program's most cherished goals.

MY COMMUNITY: MAKING A DIFFERENCE

IT IS IMPORTANT TO ME FOR PLAYERS WHO COME THROUGH THIS PROGRAM TO realize how blessed they are and that their talent is only as significant as the positive impact they make. We all need to be about the business of making life better when we have the means and opportunity. Certainly there are some causes which pull at your heartstrings more than others. I am very easily touched by causes that help individuals who need a lift or who haven't really been given a fair shake in life. I am also adamant about caring for children, for the elderly, for animals, and any other defenseless sectors of society. Anytime my vocation allows me to impact these groups, I am thrilled to help in some small way. The Lady Raider program has been involved in such community efforts as elementary school fundraising, Special Olympics, Women's Protective Services, and the South Plains Food Bank, to name a few. I feel it is part of my responsibility as a coach to teach our players to look beyond themselves to see where they can make a difference for the greater good. I was overjoyed in 2002 when Natalie Ritchie was named Big 12 Sportsperson of the Year from over 1,200 female athletes. The award honors not only her athletic prowess, but also her devotion and commitment to community service. Natalie was a frequent speaker in Lubbock area schools as well as being the

The Lady Raiders man the kids' area annually for the Komen–Lubbock Race for the Cure.

keynote speaker for several church youth groups, all the while maintaining a rigorous academic and athletic schedule. Evidence of her tremendous impact came in January 2004; she shot a record-breaking eight three-pointers in a game against Oklahoma State and the packed United Spirit Arena erupted. She is an inspiration to all of us and exemplifies the best of Lady Raider spirit.

Then there are some causes which affect you for entirely different reasons. For my staff and me, one of those is the Susan G. Komen Race for the Cure and its nationwide focus on trying to find a cure for breast cancer. There are two women who brought this challenge close to my heart. The first one is Jeannine McHaney. We lost Jeannine in the fall of 1994 after a ten-year battle with metastatic breast cancer. She hired me at Texas Tech when I had only high school coaching experience, mentored me concerning coaching at the college level, and fought many difficult battles, trying to take women's athletics to a higher level when that wasn't the popular thing to do. She told me shortly after I got the coaching job at Tech that I needed to take care of the wars on the court; she would handle everything else. She kept her word, and I tried to keep mine. It was a devastating loss when she died.

The second person is a survivor. She is my sister-in-law, Emily Sharp, one of my closest friends and married to my only brother David. She is also co-author of this book. They have two beautiful sons, Jonathan and Michael. Emily was diagnosed with breast cancer when she was 32, and their oldest son, Jonathan, was only eighteen months old. To make the story complete, you need to know that two years before, Emily had lost her 35-year-old sister, Carolyn, to the same disease. As you can imagine, our entire family was devastated by both events, and we were anxious and prayerful that Emily would be cured. After having surgery and treatment, Emily has been blessed by ten years (and counting) of good health. After her encounter, she and David welcomed a second son, Michael. Our family calls him our miracle baby.

I was so amazed and touched by Emily's courage and strength during this entire ordeal, that I wanted to be involved in something which would honor her. She actually co-founded the Lubbock Area Affiliate of the Susan G. Komen Foundation in honor of her sister and asked if I would consider being a part of it. I jumped at the chance and can tell you that through her persistence and the efforts of many other people in Lubbock, there has been over one million dollars raised in the ten years following the affiliate's inception. More importantly, many women have been educated as to the importance of preventive techniques in the fight against breast cancer. I also felt like I was able to fight back against a disease that had affected not only my personal family, but also that of the Lady Raider family through Jeannine McHaney, one of the greatest warriors in women's basketball.

Our entire team participates without fail in the Race for the Cure each fall in addition to making appearances and auctioning souvenir items from our program. More recently, our program has assisted with Kids for the Cure on Race day. Our players show up and paint children's faces, slide down an inflatable slide, and shoot some hoops with them, while their parents enjoy the Race events. Our participation has become a meaningful tradition for us in terms of community service, with the added benefit of educating our players about their own breast health.

My causes don't always become the passions of our players, and that is okay, too. I encourage them, though, to find their own causes and fight for them. There are going to be events in all of our lives that will impact us, whether negatively or positively. Some of these events will give us a passion to be committed to a cause. Instead of complaining about challenges or whining incessantly, I've found it is much more healthy to embrace them, and use your influence to do something for the greater good. If you are like me, you will always walk away more blessed than anyone. Like so many other good things that happen when people work together, everybody wins.

MY FAITH COMMITMENT: LIVING FOR GOD

I HAVE BEEN FORTUNATE TO HAVE MADE SOME GREAT FRIENDS DUE TO WOMEN'S basketball, from coaches across the country to fans from all walks of life, to

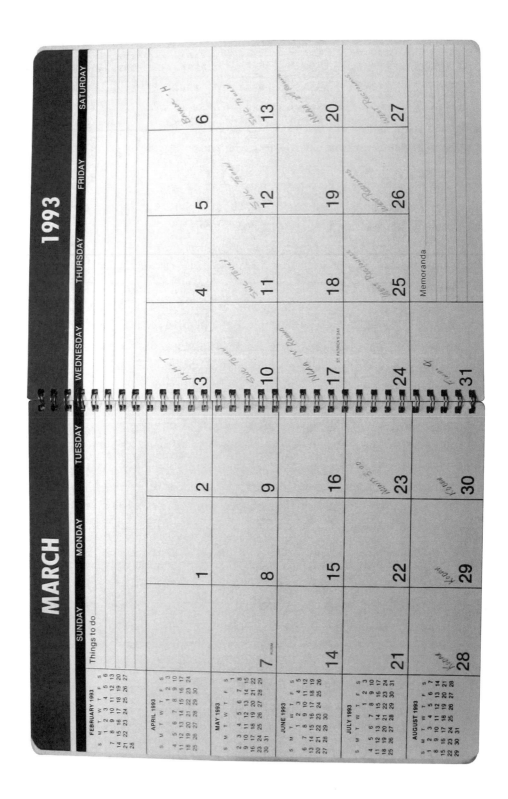

Marsha Sharp's calendar before winning the National Championship.

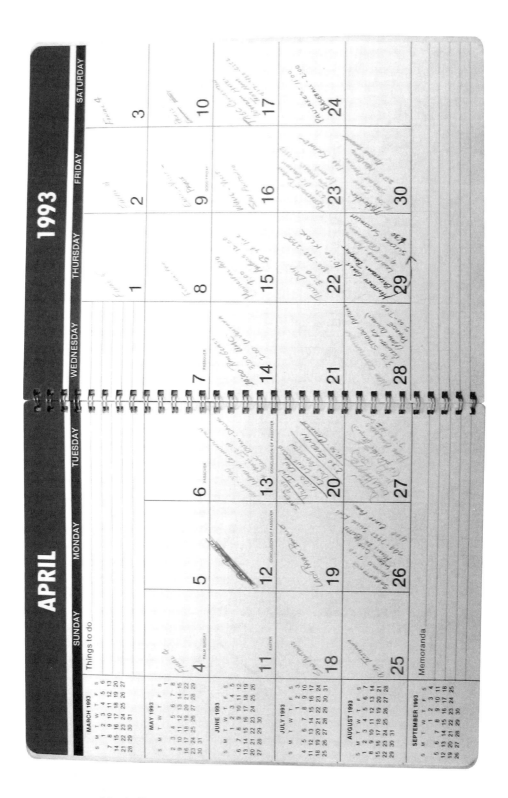

Marsha Sharp's calendar after winning the National Championship.

AN OPPORTUNITY FOR A HOPEFUL SPIRIT

Natalie Ritchie

GUARD

2000–2004

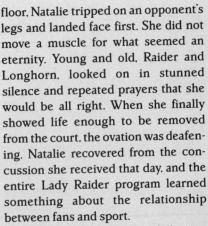

NATALIE RITCHIE WAS ELEVEN YEARS OLD when the Lady Raiders won a national championship. Krista Kirkland, her basketball icon, played on that team. Her three-point prowess, emotional leadership, and sparkling "ultimate nice gal" persona had helped catapult Texas Tech to the national spotlight. Natalie knew then what she wanted to become: a reflection of Krista Kirkland and a champion Lady Raider.

Ten years later, in the spring of 2003, when Natalie lay motionless on the floor of Reunion Arena during a Big 12 tournament game against the University of Texas, the silence of 12,000 plus fans was a testament to the realization of Natalie's early dreams. After in-bounding a ball and running at top speed down the floor, Natalie tripped on an opponent's legs and landed face first. She did not move a muscle for what seemed an eternity. Young and old, Raider and Longhorn, looked on in stunned silence and repeated prayers that she would be all right. When she finally showed life enough to be removed from the court, the ovation was deafening. Natalie recovered from the concussion she received that day, and the entire Lady Raider program learned something about the relationship between fans and sport.

Where does this fan following originate? One likely spot is the elegant fierceness of Natalie's sharp-shooting, especially from the three-point line. When she is "on," it is a thing of beauty to follow her shot from dead-on targeting, to perfect release into a perfect arc, then to net-ripping perfection time after time after time—and then there is the roar of the crowd. Her shot-making has the legendary quality of igniting a fan base and, in turn, making them a valued ally against any Lady Raider opponent. "I can feel the crowd," Natalie says. "I want to make it for them because they get the team excited. Sometimes, though, I don't notice the crowd just because I'm trying to focus so hard. There is a quiet silence that I love right before the shot goes in," she says smiling. "Then the whole place explodes." Maybe that's the silence she hears in her head when, before and after Lady Raider practices, Natalie begins at the three-point line near the baseline and begins to shoot. One, two, three, four, five shots then a giant step around the half circle to the next spot. One, two, three four, five....and on it goes until she makes her way around the entire three-point arc.

Natalie Ritchie receiving the Big 12 Sportsperson of the Year Award.

She learned, like her mentor and assistant coach, Krista Kirkland Gerlich, that the time to practice shot-making is not during practice—it's before and after practice.

The other origin of such a fan following has nothing to do with being on a basketball court. It's who Natalie is when she leaves the locker room that also inspires her team's fan base. Natalie's humble summation of being named the 2002 Sportsperson of the Year is this, "It's an award for being a nice person." Before entering high school, Natalie was home-schooled; she credits that experience with providing her an unconventional skill in relating to all ages of people. "We would take time during the school day to care for other people and try to make a habit of serving others," she explains.

This refreshing attitude is not just talk; it is what she does. Natalie heard from a fan that a 75-year-old retired teacher named Alton West was very ill with cancer and might enjoy a visit from a Lady Raider. Natalie drove to the hospital to visit him. She had taken an autographed Lady Raider poster with her and put it up in Alton's room. After a good visit, she left knowing she had made a difference, through basketball, for someone else. She was brought up to give back. According to Natalie, "This is what I've learned: win or lose, my relationship with God and serving others is what I am to be about; I am to be His hands whenever and wherever I can."

Natalie seems to understand the responsibility that comes along with greatness. "Athletes have the opportunity to touch so many lives. With the fans, it's like we have a mutual love affair and as an athlete, we're in another level of responsibility—that of community service. I have the incredible opportunity to help fans to realize the opportunity for a hopeful spirit. The worst thing for an

(Above) Natalie Ritchie gets a personalized boost from the crowd. (Left) Three-point form par excellence—Natalie Ritchie drains a bucket against Pepperdine.

athlete to have is not a big head, but a small heart."

Natalie's "mission field" is not just the fan base, but also her teammates who are recipients of encouraging notes, scriptures, and prayers throughout the season. It was Natalie's idea also to start having Thursday night team suppers. Upper classmen players get together and alternate cooking dinner for each other. It goes a long way toward building chemistry and relationships beyond basketball. Ritchie laughs, "Some of what has been cooked isn't so great, but we have a good time."

In the spring of 2004, Natalie played her final game as a Lady Raider. Even though she has no aspiration to continue playing professionally, she does believe she can use many of the lessons she learned under Coach Sharp's tutelage to make a difference in the world. "I have had this opportunity for four years. When I graduate, I'll be on another level of responsibility to my community just like Coach Sharp is. She is respected everywhere, not just at Texas Tech. She presents herself in such a classy way and communicates such a sincere, mutual respect for others. When folks look at me, I want them to say, 'This is what a Lady Raider is—a fierce competitor and a loving person.'" Ultimately, this is exactly what Coach Sharp and the Lady Raider basketball program is all about: regardless of one's profession or community, one can always provide an opportunity for a hopeful spirit.

Natalie Ritchie, Plenette Pierson and Jolee Ayers-Curry help young campers improve their game.

players I have had the joy of teaching. My life is filled with beautiful relationships; I am grateful every day for the blessing of this precious gift. The
coaching profession is a unique arena to impact lives. Walk yourself through
a series of your days, whatever your vocation may be, and you will be
amazed at the number of people who cross your path. For me, the chance to
take fifteen or so young women for a four-year period of time and provide
them an opportunity to change their lives dramatically is an amazing
endeavor. The college years typically provide the most vibrant opportunity
for change in a person's lifetime. Here students are building their own value
systems, shaping their goals, and literally trying to draw a road map for the
rest of their lives. My job as their coach is to be a guide along the way and
encourage when I can. Providing this leadership is the most important role
I play for our team. Someone said once, "Leadership is taking an individual
or group of individuals and making them do things they don't want to do in
order to take them to a place which they don't even know exists." What an
exciting and, yes, frightening, opportunity! I have spent over two decades of
my life hoping to create something very special—both for Texas Tech
University and in a small way, for the history of women's basketball. I have
been blessed to have been surrounded by great people throughout my
career. I have coached incredible young women of whom I am extremely
proud. They are actively doing wonderful things with their lives as I write
this. I have had an unbelievable experience, but I hope it is evident that,

ultimately, there is more to Marsha Sharp than a win-loss record, a group of trophies in a case, or some brass plaques on a wall.

While those are all quite special to me, they are not what drive me every day. Each one of us has to define our lives by things other than material rewards or even by how successful other people think we are. It is my experience that worldly endeavors are never going to bring us the ultimate peace and happiness that everyone wants and deserves. For me, the source of resonating peace and contentment that undergirds everything else is my Christian faith. It is this faith that teaches me my community responsibility and my life mission. It is the greatest legacy I can leave for those who come after me.

I believe that the only decision crucial for every person is what she will do with eternity, and a person's eternity begins today, with this moment. For me, the question of how I will choose to spend eternity was settled when I was ten years old in a little, pink Baptist church in Roswell, New Mexico. I gave my life to Jesus Christ and became a Christian. Every other decision I make in my life can be changed or forgiven one way or another, but this one has to be taken care of to ensure eternal life. It is humanity's ultimate question and the greatest choice we face. Becoming a Christian, however, does not mean I am close to being perfect, that I always do the right thing, or that I will never make mistakes or have regrets. It just means that I am forgiven by God's loving, mysterious, and encompassing grace.

It is important to me to work on my relationship with God all of the time. People have different ways of doing that, but for me that means believing in the power of prayer and using it, reading the ancient stories from the Bible and testing their truths in today's world, and sharing community with other Christians to strengthen my resolve. All of those factors are important to me, but the question really is how do these practices tangibly translate into every day life? What should my life really be all about?

First of all, I believe that God gives each of us talents and passions that we are to hone to excellence as positive expressions of His love. I know to the depth of my being that God expects me to use my passions for basketball, education, and young people to create situations where individual lives are affected in a dynamic way. Throughout the *Bible*, Jesus teaches that the most fulfilling experiences human beings can have involve serving others. I continue to learn in today's very complicated world that my job is not to judge what I see, but to serve as I have opportunity, following the example of the greatest community servant the world has ever known. This, then, is my ultimate goal as I approach my career and the tremendous opportunities it affords to make a difference for God.

And service doesn't end within the confines of United Spirit Arena. Outside the university, there are other opportunities to affect lives dramatically. One way is speaking to various community groups. I have kept my calendar from 1993, the year we won a national championship, and everything about Lady Raider basketball rocketed to the next level, including my opportunities to speak to various groups. Looking back at the days following that event, I had some type of speaking engagement nearly every day. The audiences have varied greatly in purpose, age, and gender. They range from Rotary Clubs, to chambers of commerce, to collections of CEOs, to elementary school luncheons, to university leadership classes, and, more recently, to a packed crowd at the Women's Hall of Fame in Knoxville, Tennessee. Having the undivided attention of several hundred people at one time is both an awesome privilege and a humbling responsibility. Even if I am talking basketball strategy with several hundred coaches, I still have the opportunity to create, or fail to create, a positive atmosphere.

One of the most amazing times we have at Texas Tech are the weeks we host summer basketball camps for young girls. These kids come in wide-eyed and in awe of everything around them. The coaches we employ from all across the region and the players who assist us probably make a bigger impression on these campers than anyone could imagine. I have had numerous young women tell me what an influence some player or coach had on them during a week of camp. Normally, about 1,500 young women run through our camps every summer. What an incredible opportunity to make a life-changing difference for the future!

Becoming involved in the lives of some of our fans is also a tremendous blessing for me. From young children who want a hug or a T-shirt to elderly people who can't wait for the season to begin, all of these friends feel like part of a larger family; our players feel the same. Traveling life's difficult roads with our fans through illness or death is an area of very special service for me. In return, they have been unbelievably supportive when troubled times have been a part of Lady Raider basketball. Celebrating with them is also a part of this special relationship.

One of the sweetest examples of this rapport came from a ten-year-old boy who happens to be an avid Lady Raider fan. We had just finished playing the first half of a game in the 2003–2004 season and were going into the locker room to discuss adjustments. I had to give some comments to a television reporter before going into the locker room, but kept hearing this little guy call my name. He said, "Coach Sharp! Coach Sharp! I have something to tell you!" I told him I would catch him when we came out to play the second half. Sure enough, when we emerged from the locker room onto the arena floor, I heard, "Coach Sharp! I have something to tell you!"

I replied, "I'm ready. What is it?"

He smiled widely and shouted above the crowd, "I'm going to be baptized!!!"   Even though I had to keep my focus on the game, I was so honored to be a part of that short, important exchange for him. I think of it often when I need to be reminded of why I'm really here.

This, then, is the bottom line for me: The opportunities we have to affect lives positively are daily staring us in the face. A friend gave me the following quote which I keep as a reminder on the corner of my desk, "Angels reveal themselves by their simple acts of kindness." Whether it's small gestures that cost us nothing or large commitments of time and money, the opportunities to make a good difference are all around us. What else could be more worthy of our time or more central to one's Christian faith? It doesn't really matter what you do for a living, how much money you make, whether you are married or single, what your gender or race is, or any other factor the world may notice— it only matters that you have a heart for service and the will to be a conduit for God's love. Some would say that the notion of giving and giving, especially when someone does not return the favor, is a foolish waste and life-draining endeavor. Our world is daily bent on getting something for something rather than giving something for nothing. I can tell you from experience that God will give you all of the strength and opportunities you have the courage to ask Him for. The greater my talents, the more responsibility I have to give back. My Christian faith tells me that this kind of giving is not an option for me; it is my happy privilege as a follower of Christ who gave his entire life for mine. The following scripture explains it best for me. May it be an inspiration to you, too, as you discover your talents, committing them to a life of service for God—for on His team, even the shortest among us can do mighty things."

"For I was hungry, and you gave me something to eat;
I was thirsty and you gave me something to drink; I was a stranger
and you invited me in; I was naked and you clothed me; I was sick
and you came to visit me; I was in prison and you came to me."

Then the righteous will answer him saying, "Lord, when did we see
you hungry and feed you, or thirsty, and give you something to drink?
And when did we see you a stranger, and invite you in, or naked and
clothe you? When did we see you sick or in prison and come to you?"

The King will answer and say to them, "Truly I say to you, to the extent
that you did it to one of the least of these my brethren, you did it to me."
Matthew 25: 35 – 40. From the New American Standard Bible

BIBLIOGRAPHY

1992-1993 Texas Tech Lady Raider National Championship Season Highlights. Mike Ogletree Productions. (Video) 1993.

Lady Raider Basketball: Leadership, Class, Integrity. Texas Tech University System News and Publications. (Video) Copyright 2002.

Sharp, Marsha. Interview by John Appicello. *The Marsha Sharp Show.* KLBK–Channel 13, Lubbock, Texas. April 5, 1993. (Video) Copyright 1993.

Texas Tech Lady Raider Media Guide 1993-1994, Walt McAlexander, Editor

Texas Tech Lady Raider Media Guides, 2002-2004 Tammi Hoffman, Editor

The following interviews were conducted by Emily F. Sharp. Those indicated with an asterisk are available as tape recordings at the Southwest Collection, Texas Tech University Library, Lubbock, Texas:

DECEMBER 2002
Erin Grant

JANUARY 2003
Carolyn Thompson-Conwright*
Michelle Thomas*
Melinda Schmucker Pharies
Stephanie Scott Gerber
Krista Kirkland Gerlich*
Sheryl Swoopes
Roger Reding
Cynthia Clinger Kinghorn*
Janice Farris Legan*
Noel Johnson
Natalie Ritchie

FEBRUARY 2003
Wanda Tyler Greenfield

MAY 2003
Linden Weese

SEPTEMBER 2003
Plenette Pierson

NOVEMBER 2003
Dr. Catherine Ronaghan

PHOTO CREDITS

Aguilar, Jaime Tomas,
Texas Tech University Daily, 101

Buckner, Joe Don, *Lubbock
Avalanche-Journal*, 13, 115, 132, 159

Cagle, Betty; 14, 16, 20, 21, 28, 73, 79,
110, 112 (top and bottom), 113, 151

Estacado High School 1991
Yearbook; 33

Hoffman, Tammi; 61

Kennedy, Norvelle; 36, 43, 51, 52,
62, 75, 90, 121, 128, 143, 157, 158

Mann, L. Scott; 68, 107, 139, 149, 156

O'Shaughnessy, Robin; *Lubbock
Avalanche-Journal*, 100

Parke, Liz; 22, 111, 114

RCL Portrait Design; 140

Sharp, Emily F.; 27, 82, 109, 145

Steinman, Sharon; 99

Texas Tech Athletics; 2, 5, 11, 30, 31,
32, 44, 45, 47, 48, 50, 56, 57, 66, 69,
84, 86, 89, 97, 98, 103, 108, 122, 124,
131, 137, 152, 160

Wayland College Trail Blazer; 9

White, Melanie; 168

WNBA; 125

Front cover images;
L. Scott Mann

Back cover image;
Joseph Victor Stefanchik,
The Dallas Morning News

INDEX

"Pseudo-team members" Linden Weese, Lance White, Vicky McKenzie, Christine Nelson, and Betty Cagle enjoy a recorded "locker room" message from Coach Sharp at the Women's Basketball Hall of Fame.

ACKNOWLEDGEMENTS

FIRST AND FOREMOST, THIS BOOK WOULD NOT HAVE HAPPENED WITHOUT THE extraordinary talents, efforts, and care of Emily Foreman Sharp. Her talent for writing continues to amaze me, and the time and energy she devoted to this book were tremendous. I am fortunate that she is my sister-in-law, but I am truly blessed that she is my friend.

The other group who took a chance on me and my story was Bright Sky Press. Rue Judd and her group are forever in my debt. I hope we will repay in a big way!

For me, this book is a compilation of lessons which have shaped my career to this point. Some of the lessons are lifelong, tried and true principles that will stay with me forever. Others are ever-changing approaches which I continue to evaluate along the way. Most of them are due to the direct influence of people who form my best quality-my very special support group. From the beginning, my parents, Charles and Mary Dell Sharp, gave me a firm foundation for the things I believe today. My dad died in 1999, but Mom continues to be a great fan. Other members of my family and a group of loyal, bright, and understanding friends inspire and encourage me daily. They cheer me on when things are great, but more importantly they surround and protect when things are not so good. They make my life complete.

My staff's talents, energies, and loyalty are unsurpassed in this profession. Their innumerable strengths cover my weaknesses, and their experience allows me to pursue other endeavors such as coaching a USA basketball team, serving as the President of the Women's Basketball Coaches Association, or writing a book. This book is as much about them as it is me.

The main reason I wanted to write this is to honor all of the great young women who have played in this program. The stories included here are a mere sampling of the way each player has made her unique impact on Lady Raider Basketball. They are why I work everyday and they are really the story. Lady Raiders will always be my lifelong friends.

The fans of Texas Tech Women's Basketball are called the Lady Raider Nation. There is a reason for that. If you want to experience the greatest fans in the country, I invite you to take a seat in the United Spirit Arena during one of our home games and witness an enthusiasm as wide as the West Texas horizon.

Most important of all, I thank God for always being with me along this amazing journey. To be in this very special place at this very special time is a great gift and is clear evidence of His love for me. In the end, this journey is all that really matters.